What This Book is About and Who Should Read It

This book is written primarily for investors and voters – people who are sick of reading company or political reports about expensive project failures, and who know that it is they who will ultimately be the losers. It is a brief account of the main abuses and areas of incompetence, and offers suggestions of how to hold politicians and company directors accountable to eliminate waste and exploitation; how to stop daylight robbery by opportunistic executives, foil expensive and under-performing project contractors, and maybe prevent the next economic or environmental calamity.

Historical man-made disasters can be grouped by a few characteristic causes, and in particular:

- ignorance, especially when doing something novel,
- negligence; and
- greed, including taking excessive risk in the hope of enrichment.

Projects involve spending money, often on a vast scale. They also often involve doing something novel and taking risks. Mix these ingredients up with a global business environment driven by greed, and a global political environment dominated by self-serving opportunists, and we have all the makings of disaster. Major events may draw attention, but there are very many other project losses that are little publicised. These less spectacular abuses add up to billions of dollars of investors' and taxpayers' money annually wasted or lost to project pirates. The failures include project delays, over-expenditure and under-performing end products – new industries, mines, oilfields and public works that just don't come up to expectations, sometimes abysmally so.

One of the basic techniques of safety and loss management comes from the observation that for every major accident or loss, there are many more smaller incidents. Create an environment where there are few minor incidents, and there will also be fewer major losses. Nip all abuse in the bud: concentrate on the thousands of apparently lesser aspects of project abuse or incompetence, and major losses will also be rooted out.

To understand how to avoid abuses and losses, you have to understand how pirates operate and how negligence and deception go undetected. That in turn requires examination of some of the basics of project management methodology. And, yes, you guessed it, many of the abuses are caused by project executives and contractors, who may happily collect huge bonuses for actually impoverishing the project owner, the shareholder or the taxpayer.

PREVENTING PROJECT PIRACY

An Investor's and Voter's Primer on How to Avoid Being Fleeced by Project Abuses

PETER WATERMEYER

Publication history

Printed by CreateSpace, an Amazon.com company, 2012

Also available as an e-book

ISBN-13: **978-1468044072** (CreateSpace-Assigned)
ISBN-10: **1468044079**

Disclaimer

The characters, companies and institutions named or described in this book are all fictional and do not relate to any specific person, company or institution.

ACKNOWLEDGEMENT

I am indebted to Anthony Nanson for his conscientious and critical editing of this book, which has resulted in many improvements in readability and grammar. However, our styles and perspectives differ, and the end result is entirely my own responsibility.

For Margie

Oh, better far to live and die
Under the brave black flag I fly,
Than play a sanctimonious part,
With a pirate head and a pirate heart.
Away to the cheating world go you,
Where pirates all are well-to-do.

W.S. Gilbert, 1879

Contents

Contents

Introduction

This book is mainly about complex and expensive projects and the abuses and poor performance that may occur in their creation and execution. A project in this context is the execution of a plan to achieve a defined objective, and the plans are for major investments such as building new factories, mines or transport systems.

This book is also concerned with the behaviour and practices of people charged with managing other people's assets – money, resources, enterprises, projects. For the sake of simplicity, these people will be referred to as 'Executives'[3], but the issues can be as applicable to the employment of executive directors, 'expert' consultants, management companies and senior government officials as they are to corporate managers. All these people are paid to do a job, and so there has to be a person or entity to which they are accountable. This is often a board of directors or state hierarchy, representing the asset-owning entity or shareholders, and will usually be referred to here as 'the Owner'. For simplicity, the person or entity overseeing the Owner's interests will be referred to as 'the Director' (generally excluding executive directors or company presidents, who cannot be considered impartial guardians of the Owner's interests).

In the examples which follow, the underlying cause of many problems is that when performing their official duties, executives tend not to behave the same as when dealing with their personal assets. Their thought processes are different, and so are their ethical standards. The same applies to many of the other project performers.

The behaviour of a wide spectrum of people and entities is in question here. At one extreme is the downright criminal executive or official, whose main purpose is to get rich by fraud or malpractice. The other

---

3 When a role has been specifically defined like this, I will employ an initial capital. When the same word is used in the general sense there will be no capital.

end of the spectrum includes those who are compromising or not making the best use of resources and opportunities, without even realising it. In between the extremes, there are many executives who keep within the legal requirements of service to their employer while prioritising the advancement of their own interests wherever possible. 'Their own interests' are not necessarily financial, and may well relate more to their ego and their status in an organisation. My main intentions are to indicate how Owners (including shareholders) should ensure that their Directors and well-intentioned Executives avoid questionable project practices, and to expose the practices of Executives and others who have unacceptable objectives that ultimately impoverish us all.

The focus of this book is projects, and in particular large projects and large organisations. However, much of what it covers is also applicable to the on-going management of an enterprise.

For sheer management effectiveness, there is nothing to beat the situation of one-man (or woman[4]) enterprise owner-developers, who have the full authority and responsibility for what they do, carry all the gains or consequences personally and have a full grasp of the whole enterprise. I have little advice here for this kind of enterprise, if it sets up and performs its own projects. However, there is always a limiting size and complexity, or a breadth of ownership, beyond which the enterprise cannot be managed in that way. Even for owner-managed enterprises, a large project represents an attractive sector of the business for delegated management, because superficially it seems to be easy to create accountability by the setting of defined targets and the imposition of reporting systems for performance measurement. Superficially, it seems to be easy.

In general, with increased size and complexity of operation, there arises need for a structure in which leading specialists are employed for the operational functions, and the overall leadership becomes more of a strategic director and Owner's representative than a hands-on manager. The larger and more complex the enterprise, the greater the need for general management skills rather than expert specialists at the top.

---

4   Throughout this text, 'man' and 'he' should please be taken to include 'woman' and 'she', purely to avoid the occasional literary clumsiness of being gender-inclusive. Please understand man in the sense of mankind. The same applies to such words as 'chairman', 'manager', 'businessman' and 'contractor'.

'Projects' – capital developments for which scope, budget and timetable can be defined – are a natural choice for management by a specialist group not engaged in the day-to-day management of a business, even of one that has not evolved to the point of control by a board of directors.

Sometimes we need to remind ourselves that to define a parcel of business as a 'project' is fundamentally just a form of management practice. This management practice has inherent advantages of management focus, accountability and specialisation, but from the viewpoint of the whole enterprise all the work done and money expended on the project remain an integral part of the enterprise and must be fully integrated with the enterprise's other on-going work. In many respects, and certainly in the setting of objectives and the standards of acceptability of work, the business of the project and the functioning of the overall enterprise should be the same. As an example, consider the following case of a project carried out by a mining company to open up a new mine.

To decide whether and how to go ahead with the project, a study needs to be conducted. Theoretically, and especially in the case of a hugely attractive opportunity requiring fast implementation, this could be a cursory business plan. (But watch out – sometimes very important negative aspects can be overlooked.) However, that is seldom the case. In general, the requirement for due diligence on behalf of the investors is that the study be very thorough.

There are some very specific study requirements; for instance, having learnt from the experience of a massive fraud, the Toronto Stock Exchange requires a detailed report in accordance with a demanding format (NI 43101). Though mainly aimed at the verification and certification of mineral resources, this also requires a full investigation of all operational factors, such as mineral recovery plant performance, product marketing and taxation, all drawn together into an economic performance evaluation. In this mining instance and in general, the study must evaluate the full lifetime performance of the projected enterprise, including its eventual decommissioning, and all associated risks. To do this, it is necessary to produce an outline design, costing and performance evaluation of not just the physical items to be purchased and constructed, but also all the intended operational methodology, such as mine and factory operation and product marketing. The complete business. If the study conclusions warrant it, and if the project is authorised and funded, there follow two phases: a project phase, in which the basic management task is to perform the capital investment as planned (or better); and an operational phase, in which the task is to operate the business as planned (or better). Any over– or under-performance from the first phase, including the setting of targets of performance, is automatically carried over into the second phase.

To treat a parcel of an enterprise's business as a project is therefore fundamentally an exercise of management practice. Definition of a part of a business or government service as a project with specific completion targets enables the use of a compendium of developed methodologies that have proved indispensable to good performance.

Here are some major issues that arise:

- As we have noted, the project conception and execution process has to be set up and maintained in a way that exactly follows the needs of the whole enterprise. Since the project function is a limited part of the enterprise, it is necessary to guard against 'sub-optimisation'. This includes avoiding practices by which the project becomes an end in itself, such that any conflicts with other enterprise objectives get decided in favour of the project management, to the overall detriment of the larger enterprise. It is similarly necessary to ensure that the project management – including the Executives and staff responsible, and major external contractors and consultants – are engaged in such a way that sub-optimisation be minimised.

- More narrowly, the project management function needs to be made to set suitably ambitious and competitive targets that it can be held accountable for meeting. Otherwise, the whole enterprise will be rendered less competitive, or in the case of a government department taxpayers' money will be wasted. Target-setting is compromised if a single project execution director or management company is responsible for both the conceptualisation which sets the targets and achieving them. In that event, you can expect the target to include some pretty useful contingencies (of cash, time and performance standard), often well hidden. There has to be some competition or external critical evaluation to set sufficiently challenging targets that correspond to the best project performance.

The opposite practice – the setting of project objectives that are inherently unachievable – must also be avoided. This situation arises especially in politically motivated projects and where the benefits of company flotation depend upon an 'optimistic' view being taken. It can come about when the responsible Executives give way to pressure from important parties with private objectives, including predatory shareholders (about which more will follow), and especially if those Executives' terms of office expire before the time when the consequences come home to roost. The greater the project size and the longer its duration, the greater may be the temptation to set an over-optimistic target to get the project go-ahead. The over-optimism usually relates to cost, but it may also relate to time schedule or technical functionality, or even all three of these. The initial optimism is often followed by over-optimistic performance reporting for a long period, after which the perpetrators may avoid the eventual consequences of under-performance one way or another.

In the case of a project execution contractor, there can be many ways of 'getting off the hook' from an unrealistic project target after gaining some up-front benefits of participation. For instance, the contractor may wait until the project is so far advanced that for the Owner to change contractors would be unacceptably chaotic and expensive. At this point the contractor demands a renegotiation of contract terms on pain of stopping work. The contractor needn't resort to naked blackmail; he just says 'I can't afford to carry on.' He might be even more subtle than that, by suddenly reducing the intensity of work, then 'confessing' to financial problems. He will often try to confuse the issue, before the crisis arrives, by generating a lot of unjustified claims for extra payment and requests to lower the standards of delivery, and when these are turned down, complaining bitterly about being ruined by the Owner's unreasonable attitude.

It should be apparent to the reader that it need not be a contractor who behaves in this fashion. Similar behaviour may be exhibited by the enterprise's own executives, except they will likely fall back on some constraints they've had to work under. These may include internal bureaucracy, a delay before the Board approved the project, distractions caused by other priorities, or a blurring of responsibilities following management reorganisation. In the event that disclosure of really serious failure becomes unavoidable, reorganisation may be taken to a 'strategic' level where entire companies are restructured and reformed to disguise individual accountability. Government departments have an even easier time if they fail, as they have no competitors to set a standard of performance. Denial of failure is reasonably easy, and without competitors to contradict them, they can blame just about anyone except themselves.

- In the context of a project to turn around an existing business, a common death knell for the enterprise is the stripping of assets saleable over book value to produce an illusion of financial improvement, at which point the management perpetrator decamps with his bonuses.

- For new production facilities, the project's apparent financial and schedule performance can often be enhanced, up to and well past the commissioning stage, by disregarding some of the costs and risks relating to future plant operation and maintenance.

Many similar project practices are available to the unscrupulous Executive (or government) wanting to make the present look rosier at the cost of future expense or risk, which is hidden or understated or insufficiently emphasised. I shall describe some of these in later chapters.

The situations and practices mentioned above occur all too frequently in major enterprises, corporations and government departments. Often the Directors blind themselves that 'that couldn't happen here'. It always does; it is a part of human nature. The only issue is: how well are such behaviour and its consequences limited? This then is a challenge to the Directors – how to keep the project Executives and execution specialists in check, including the age-old question of *Quis custodes custodiet?*

The challenge calls on the developed skills of a Director's experience, including such abstract capabilities as intuitive ability to recognise personality and predict errant personal behaviour. It also often calls on the willingness of the critical Director to expose himself to opposition, including abuse and ridicule, in a field where he may not be confident.

Embracing so many different types of business operation and situation, this is a wide subject that does not easily lend itself to simple directives and checklists. I have called this book a 'primer' in order to emphasise its necessary incompleteness in the face of so many differing situations. Despite these limitations, from what I have observed, many major project failures could have been averted if only some of the malpractices that will be described here had been prevented by a critical Board of Directors or Owner's representative. What I regard as 'failures' include many instances where project targets were set too low: the project may have achieved the target, but in the long run the enterprise was left with a less competitive resource. A project Executive or execution contractor may have been fêted on conclusion of the project, but later the business stagnated or went bust, or the nation was left with higher taxation for less service delivery.

Turning to ways to curtail abuse, although the Board of Directors' responsibilities are the same for projects and ongoing business, the way of exercising Board oversight cannot usually be the same, for two fundamental reasons:

- Project performance is measured and reported in a quite different way from the performance of the ongoing business; and
- Projects are often long term in nature, and what happens in one month is usually quite different from the next month.

Although sophisticated measurement and reporting methodologies have been developed to assess performance as a project progresses, actual performance is too often misunderstood or misrepresented until too late for effective Board action. Often the root cause of eventual underperformance and its late recognition goes right back to the way the project was set up in the first place. Much of this book will examine the causes of such problems and consider possible remedies.

In general, I have avoided the use of named examples of what I consider to have been inadequate performance, failure and malpractice. I am bound by considerations of confidentiality and also do not wish to incur any litigation by parties that may feel offended. I have named no real names and have sometimes scrambled or relocated incidents of abuse. I believe that the readers to whom this book is mainly addressed will already have had quite enough adverse experiences to understand that the problems are real and to critically appraise the salience of what I have to say. We are addressing some very serious forms of economic rot here, and the rot can equally affect both capitalist and socialist systems.

In conclusion, I have set out in this book to describe:

- some of the more important avenues by which projects may be abused or poorly performed, in the context of standard project management methodology;
- safeguards that may be employed to protect the interests of investors, including questions to be asked about project justification, set-up, execution and reporting;
- suggestions – not necessarily original – on how regulating and governance bodies should structure overview to prevent abuse and promote the investors' interests.

Ultimately, of course, it's up to investors and voters to insist on adequate safeguards. Here are some yardsticks to gauge the strength of the protection.

Part I. Where Pirates Prey

1. Management by Incentive

Inadequate Incentive Formulation

The Introduction began with the comment that one of the underlying causes of many of the problems here addressed is that executives in their corporate roles tend not to behave the same as when dealing with their own personal assets. A fundamental issue immediately arises: how to encourage the required behaviour, attitudes and, ultimately, performance?

On a tour of the walls of Jerusalem several years ago, the Palestinian guide pointed out to me 'the Engineer's tomb'. The Engineer, he said, had been hanged on the spot by the visiting Sultan because of inadequate construction progress. This was undoubtedly an effective way of discouraging poor project management, but it seems that such practice is no longer socially acceptable. In modern management thinking, the basic enterprise or project Owner's tool is the 'management incentive'.

The structure and application of such incentives is therefore a starting point for this commentary. Indeed, it is also one of the finishing points, many of the intermediate subjects being aimed at recognising what behaviour and performance should be required, how it can be defined and measured, and consequently how to formulate the incentives. 'Incentive' is used here in its most general sense, as a motivating factor, some means of encouraging the accomplishment of a desired outcome. It need not be a financial incentive.

In this chapter, we will consider some of the general issues around incentives. These issues will be developed in detail in subsequent chapters.

Some rather obvious issues need to be addressed first, for the sake of completeness. To be effective, the incentive must be credible. We are talking about incentivising experienced leaders, not a bunch of amateurs. They are unlikely to be fully motivated by anything less than a binding commitment, specifying exactly what incentive will be furnished upon reaching what target. They will not be motivated by the setting of an unachievable or hardly achievable target, or one whose achievement could be too easily frustrated by circumstances outside their control. The incentive will not seem credible to the executives unless the target is clearly one from which the Owner will derive benefits significantly greater than the value of the incentives paid out, thus assuring the executives of the Owner's support in meeting the targets.

The most common failure in setting incentives seems to be that the 'target' is set too narrowly. The extreme case of this is to formulate the target in money terms only, especially if rewards are offered for relatively short-term gains. Unbelievable though it seems, such practice appears to have been widespread in banking and financial management corporations and to have played no small part in the financial crisis of 2008. Senior executives and entire corporations seem to have been incentivised to achieve short-term financial targets without sufficient qualification, as might be imposed in a strict regulatory environment. In this case, the most significant missing target qualification was that of risk. From the pirates' point of view, it paid handsomely to take excessive risks to make high short-term profits and get paid marvellous bonuses. If – and in the longer term if becomes when – the risks materialise into substantial losses, the losing debt-owners will – and did – find themselves in the position of the creditor being informed by his debtor that *we* have a problem. Result: Pirates 1, Corporate Governance 0.

There are three important lessons to be drawn here.

- The incentives must match evenly and in full the long-term objectives of the Owner, be it the owner of the enterprise or the owner of debt, the investor or the lender.

- The assumption of risk should be exactly understood by the Owners and lenders, and no further risk permitted without their sanction.
- The incentive scheme must not permit a situation to arise where, having failed to meet the objectives adequately, failed Executives or contractors are simply able to renegotiate their situation because without their ongoing participation the Owner will be in even worse trouble.

Because of these and other considerations, Directors overseeing the implementation of a project have some important fields of action for policing the incentives offered to the project Executive, and any other potential beneficiaries:

- **Definition**
  Ensure that both the project and its method of implementation are completely defined and that all aspects of this definition match the long-term needs of the broader enterprise or Owner.
- **Complete Performance**
  Ensure that the proposed incentives cannot be earned without meeting all the objectives of the project, and the needs of the Owner. (Note: 'all' means 100%. If, say, 80% still merits a significant incentive payment, the Executive may be tempted to sacrifice the 20% of more demanding objectives and concentrate attention on the less demanding.)
  Challenging Target
  Ensure that the standards of management performance tied to any incentive scheme are independently verified to be adequately challenging.
- **Risk Management**
  Ensure that adequate risk analysis has been performed and that the project is executed in accordance with an approved risk management plan. (Note: the risk analysis and management plan does not just apply to the duration of the project. It must address the whole operational lifetime of the project works, including the eventual decommissioning of plant and winding-up of a business.)

3

- **Consequences of Failure**
  Ensure that there is a plan to avoid the situation whereby a failed Executive or other project performer is able to renegotiate terms following under-performance, or simply walk away from a mess without severe penalty.
- **Independent Assessment**
  Ensure that the measurement of performance is carried out by a credible independent system, or stringent overview of the project reporting system, to avoid measurement bias.

The following chapters will enlarge on all these subjects and recommend the means of 'ensuring'.

Contracted Projects

A basic form of project performance incentive is the competitive tender and contract, including one or a small number of contracts to carry out the project. The instrument of competition is used to obtain the best deal for the Owner. In so far as the contract binds the contractor to the required standard of performance, and the only way he can make a profit is by efficient performance, making a profit and avoiding a loss becomes the driving incentive. This standard approach comes with its own challenges, and these will be discussed later, with the exception of one: the Owner remains critically dependent on another party, the Owner's Executive, to set up the contract and manage the contractor. There is still a project Executive to be policed as outlined above. The need to incentivise and police the Project Executive remains just as critical to getting the best value. Just because a contractor has been appointed by a successfully competitive process does not imply that all is well; it is a necessary but not a sufficient condition.

The Project Accountability and Incentive Chain

For the most part, we are dealing with 'accountability-structured' incentives here. This means that the incentive corresponds to defined responsibilities, targets and therefore accountability. The chain of incentives follows exactly the structure of accountability, and its dynamics and effectiveness are analysed in terms of that structure. 'Lateral incentives', rewards given for a contribution (usually a suggestion) outside the rewarded individual's or entity's defined responsibilities, are also important in some situations. Such schemes also have to be carefully structured to avoid abuse and encourage only the desired behaviour.

The chain of incentives starts with the Owner of the project, the entity paying for its delivery. The Owner has to decide what he wants: how he does this and articulates it are critical issues, to be reviewed in Chapter 3. The Owner's main interest may be the long-term profitability of a business or the long-term service offered by a community facility. Or the emphasis may be on a short– to medium-term increase in share value, or a relatively quick political benefit. This will also lead us to consider the situation of the predatory shareholder. It is not my present intention to debate the social acceptability of the Owner's purpose; I emphasise only that the purpose should be clearly defined and communicated. Call it the enterprise 'Mission Statement' if you like.

Next, in order to analyse the dynamics of motivation and incentivation, we can identify a few roles or functions relating to the project:

A. The executive or group of executives primarily charged with defining or approving the definition of the project, whom we will call 'the Definer'.

B. The executive(s) responsible for setting the project performance targets, whom we will call 'the Goalsetter'.

C. The leading executive responsible for achieving the project performance targets, whom we defined before as 'the Executive'.

D. The Director, to whom the Executive is accountable. This role was defined before, but be reminded that this may be a board of directors, a panel of non-executive directors, a government hierarchy, etc.

E. The 'Owner's Engineer', responsible for engineering and drafting the contract documentation, including the definition of the project works, the performance requirements and the contract commercial conditions.

F. The person who monitors the measurement and reporting of all aspects of project performance, and reports the comparison with defined target performance, whom we will call 'the Evaluator'. Financial audit is included in but is only a part of this role; the value of what is being delivered (but has yet to be completed to a point where it will affect financial performance) and the conformance to expectations also have to be measured. These performance expectations can be expressed in financial terms and rolled up as a lifetime financial forecast spreadsheet summed up to a single net present value (NPV), but updated risk, safety and environmental assessment should also be considered. More on these matters follows in subsequent chapters.

G. The 'Project Manager', responsible to the Executive for achieving the project performance targets. He or she usually heads a staff of project management specialists.

H. The Contractor, paid to execute the project work and hand over the completed product to the Owner, in accordance with a contract negotiated with and subject to the supervision of the Project Manager.

The roles may be structured as separate accountable entities; or they may be combined in various ways, and to some extent usually are. Some typical combinations:

1. The Definer A, the Goalsetter B and the Evaluator F are all the responsibility of the Executive, C. C is then responsible to the Director D (which may be a board of directors) for setting the project targets, and for measuring and reporting their progressive achievement.

2. The Project Manager G and the Owner's Engineer E are all part of a staff department reporting to the Executive C.

3. The Project Manager G, the Owner's Engineer E and many of the project team are part of a staff department (reporting to the Executive C) which carries out many of the functions, and especially the technical ones, of the project. They contract out the remainder of the work in a number of relatively fragmented contracts and purchases.

4. Combination of 1 and 3 above. The Executive C is now solely responsible for all aspects of the project, including its detailed execution, the setting of goals and the measurement of performance.

5. As for 3, except that the functions of the Project Manager G and Owner's Engineer E are now carried out by a turnkey or management contractor, or a few such entities, and the project is executed by another Contractor H.

6. As for 5, but the pre-project work of the Owner's Engineer E and the project management and execution G are both performed by a single contracting company. This becomes particularly dangerous if the Contractor H is allowed to assume too much of the role of the Goalsetter B or the Evaluator F, and is not critically challenged in this regard.

In a small organisation, many of the roles have to be combined for the organisation to remain competitive, but we are looking at large organisations and projects here. A fundamental issue is that often the existence of inherently separable and potentially conflicting roles is not recognised, and so an individual or entity can become by default the arbiter of interests conflicting with his own; can become both gamekeeper and poacher. He can set the project goals, control the project execution and control the way in which project performance is measured and reported.

An organisation may be set up in many ways to suit its purpose. The preceding analysis, which I call a 'project accountability and performance structure' analysis, has to be modified in each organisational context. This is an essential prerequisite for setting incentives for the best-balanced result for the whole enterprise – or, even without consideration of incentives, for setting up project responsibilities and accountabilities in the best way for the organisation rather than for the senior individuals and contractors who are employed.

It is not necessary to elaborate the potential for conflict of interest when any of these roles are combined, as they often are as per the examples given. I want only to make clear that some responsibilities can conflict, and to urge the Director, confronted with any particular combination, to enquire how any conflicts have been resolved. If no satisfactory answer is available, the Director can conclude that the organisation is not structured to get best value out of its role-players.

I have experience of many Executives who would trash even the concept of such an analysis. Naturally. Who would wish to be called to account, if he can instead set his own performance standards and control his own verdict on whether even these selective standards have been met?

Before considering any practical application of such analysis, it is necessary to explore various aspects of project process which the analysis should govern.

2. Is the Project Really Justified? Initial Considerations

Project Authorisation Criteria

Any private enterprise, any government needs projects, or it will ultimately stagnate. Projects are always needed; the decision on whether a project is justified must not only be based on evaluating it in isolation, but also address the usual need to allocate limited resources to the most potentially beneficial projects, and ensure that projects are conceived in the best possible way.

Thus there are three questions to be asked, not only (1) 'Is this a good or an acceptable project?' but also (2) 'Is it the right project?' and (3) 'Are we going about it in the right way?' The second and third questions are comparative. To answer them properly usually requires a lot of work, including diligent development and assessment of various alternatives that may ultimately not be pursued. Such work is often not done properly, especially in the case of major or political projects that have been allowed to become an end in themselves, and especially when there is pressure to economise on pre-project expenditure.

Sometimes, chief executives or ministers allow themselves to become over-committed to a project in terms of reputation or emotion. In the last few decades, the corporate and government ruinous projects of choice have been over-the-top information technology (IT) projects, which have ended up costing far beyond estimate and have functioned poorly (though their champions seldom admitted it). But there has also been plenty of more traditional wastage, such as projects to expand industries that appeal to traditions or to employment aspirations which are impractical dreams rather than reality. These include developments in desert areas that should realistically have been left as deserts; factories to make products that are no longer competitive; mines that could not economically be mined; environmental protection projects that, when all is considered, actually damage the environment more than protect it; lavish hosting of games that will be forgotten while the pain of the debt incurred and of lost alternative opportunities remains.

If (non-executive) Directors are presented with projects for approval without a critical examination of alternatives, their Board should be regarded as dysfunctional. Further, the development of a major project to the point where it is ready for final authorisation is usually a matter of years. If the Board has little oversight of the development process – which is when alternatives are considered – it will not be in a good position to ensure that all the issues of comparative opportunity and alternative means of implementation have been properly considered. A Board meeting is usually too late a stage to intervene; critical directors may be coerced on the basis that any delay will be harmful to the proposed project or to its objectives.

Commercial Projects
Commercial projects are generally easily evaluated in terms of net-present-value (NPV) analysis or internal rate of return (IRR). Some observations on these analyses will be presented later, but it is important to note that such financial analysis is only one, a necessary but not sufficient criterion for gauging the attractiveness of the project.

Let us consider three broader issues:

- Potential impact on wider interests of the business, including negatives such as adverse customer and public perceptions, and positives such as the growth of the enterprise's competence during project execution, and the further application of the acquired competence to other operations of the enterprise.
  Clearly, what should be considered is the impact on the entire enterprise – or country, in the case of a major national project. To do this effectively requires the production and comparison of

complete models of the enterprise or country with and without the implementation of the project. The financial analysis is only a part of this.

The extent to which such a wide-ranging comparative analysis is available, and is comprehensive, may be taken by the Director as an indication of the acceptability of the project authorisation process. As outlined previously, there is little value in pointing out such deficiency at the time that the project is presented for authorisation. The time to exercise oversight is during the pre-feasibility and feasibility study stage.

- Have all the opportunities been evaluated, recorded and presented which arise from a wide-ranging analysis of the consequences of project implementation? Who is going to gain incidental benefit from the project? Are such people and interests, by happy coincidence, in any way related to the project's protagonists? Will the investors in the project receive appropriate benefit from these lateral opportunities?

- Risk is always a major issue when evaluating project justification. Some of the more detailed issues will be considered later. At the overview level:
  - There is a risk of faulty information and a faulty process used to justify, define and set up the project.
  - There is a risk of project execution failure.
  - There is usually any number of operational risks, following project completion.

Risk management procedures have been widely institutionalised in recent years, and it can by now be expected as a matter of course that a thorough risk assessment will be carried out by a competent party. Herein lies a new danger: such risk assessments can be so lengthy and incomprehensible to general readers that they become practically irrelevant. A report format should be insisted upon in which there is a concise executive summary that assesses all the major risks and proposes corresponding mitigation measures, with no 'on the one hand … and on the other'. The remainder of the report should be strictly for back-up reference, in case of a need to challenge or elaborate the basis for the recommendations.

In all reports to be used for project justification, Directors should carefully scrutinise disclaimers and limitations of liability. Often consultants will claim that it is unreasonable to accept liability for errors that could result in major project losses, when their fee is a small fraction of that amount. It may be so; it usually is. In regard to this risk and indeed all potentially damaging risks, the Director should enquire whether insurance is available. If insurance is not available or is considered to be prohibitively expensive, is this not an indication that an unreasonable gamble is being taken?

Political or Government Projects

The justification of government projects should be subject to exactly the same oversight as those of private enterprise, in fact more so, as here the Executive is about as far removed from the Owner (i.e. the citizens) as it can be, with consequent loss of direct concern for the money spent. The possibility of corruption, in all its forms from unfair advantage to gross criminality, is ever present.

An inability to perform a realistic cost–benefit analysis should seldom be considered acceptable. Failure to do this acceptably can and does lead to money being wasted on inappropriate facilities in inappropriate locations. In exactly the same way as for private enterprises, it is necessary to analyse a model of the complete social and economic systems involved, or to get as close to this ideal as possible. In fact all of the considerations listed above apply, but some issues require special emphasis.

For instance, it should be unacceptable to justify a project for the provision of drinking water simply on the basis that people need water to drink. Should the people be at the place where water is needed at all? Should they rather be accommodated elsewhere? If water is provided in the present location, what other subsidies will be required in the long run, and what will be the overall economic benefits to justify this expenditure?

Privatisation, or the potential to privatise services otherwise rendered by a government, can create a competitive benchmark and therefore be a valuable tool for gauging the cost–effectiveness of government services. Some issues of ensuring that the comparison is valid will be considered later, in the broader context of contracted-out services and facilities. In the present context, the main observations to be made are that

A. If there is no interest in competing to offer privatised services, this may be an indication that the government is charging too little for the provision of the services. Or the service may be found to be a very efficient government unit, whose management should be copied elsewhere.

B. If there is great interest in providing privatised services, this may be an indication of government inefficiency or over-charging. Unless there are over-riding considerations such as security, it must surely be to the national advantage to have some of each type of government-rendered service provided privately in competition with the state authorities, as a performance yardstick. However, the privatisation process, like outsourcing in an industrial context, brings with it several opportunities for piracy which will be considered later.

Projects to promote employment and provide welfare cannot be excluded from full critical consideration of all possible alternatives and ramifications, simply because they are seen as inherently worthy causes. It is vital to analyse a realistic macro-model to ensure that optimum solutions are adopted.

Before considering project justification in more detail, it is necessary to consider the definition of the project to be analysed.

3. Defining the Project

Scope, Quality, Cost and Time

From the considerations of the previous chapters, it should be evident that the authorisation of funds for an insufficiently defined project is liable to be a licence for the project executive to print money.

A project is conveniently presented in terms of four components which often conflict with each other: scope, quality, cost and time. Many management schools combine scope and quality under the heading of 'technical acceptability'. This practice is not recommended, as some important aspects may then be insufficiently emphasised, in particular economic and financial issues relating to post-project operation. More on these follows.

Without a full description of all four components, a project is inadequately defined and its performance cannot be held to proper account.

Scope defines what is included in the project, and in particular its purpose. The definition of scope must incorporate all items that (a) are needed to achieve a defined long-term purpose, (b) incur a cost and (c) are in any other way required for complete project delivery. In any IRR or NPV analysis, as described in the next chapter, items of operational cost or delayed items of capital cost must be taken into account. Although these are taken at appropriately discounted value, their value can be large. Note that for many of the items that may be needed to achieve the purpose, there is no hard and fast rule as to what should be included (and delivered) as part of the project scope. Many items or activities can be excluded from 'the project' and be furnished as part of 'operational expenditure'. An item of extra capital expenditure within the 'project' can reduce an 'operational expense', and the lack of capital expenditure can have the reverse effect. Examples will follow.

Quality is essentially a qualification of scope, in which standards of construction, performance and durability are defined, as are also the surveillance, testing and inspection requirements to ensure that the standards are met.

For project authorisation and control purposes, cost should not be presented as a single figure, unless discounted to present-day values, a process that in itself gives rise to uncertainties about the appropriate discount rate. Cost is a function of time, a negative cash flow over a period when interest may be paid or gained. Cost is usually dependent on various indeterminate issues such as exchange rate fluctuation, inflation, and market uncertainties. It can only be accurate historically; as the project progresses, future costs are periodically re-estimated and the cost forecast is updated, thereby initiating management action to attempt to remedy any overspending.

Time to completion is likewise seldom a single elapsed period or date. Progress against schedule needs to be subjected to re-estimate, updated forecast and initiation of remedial action in the same way as cost. Often there is a phased completion, as a productive facility or a road or housing scheme is brought from initial operation into full operation. Sometimes it is possible to perform part of the required work before project authorisation, if the risk of non-authorisation is accepted and funds are available. There is no hard and fast definition of the allocation of work, especially investigative and intellectual work, between the project and the study work that precedes the authorisation of the project.

Given all the inevitable elasticities in the definition of the project and its performance parameters, it should be apparent that to talk of a major project costing X amount and being completed in Y months is usually a gross over-simplification, which can lead to false evaluations of performance and false comparisons. And yet such simplification is very common.

We will in future chapters look in more detail at some of these issues of the definition of the project and its performance. At this point, there follow examples of possible weaknesses in definition which are often exploited by project Executives wishing to create leeway to make project performance look better than it is, or to make projects look more attractive to the potential investor than is actually justified.

The most usual deception is to make the (initial) capital outlay a stand-alone measure of project performance, while neglecting possible negative performance aspects that impair operating performance or incur additional capital cost later. Sometimes justification for this is made with a vague statement that 'once the plant (or facility) is up and running, there will naturally be a number of performance-enhancing projects paid for out of production revenue'. That can be a justifiable way to operate, although often the costs of modifying an operating facility are much more expensive than including the right feature initially, even when stated in 'real' terms that allow for inflation . The critical Director should ensure that the claimed facility operating performance matches the scope and quality included within the project. If the predicted operating performance is based on factorised data rather than on the actual designs included, then conduct a detailed calculation of the operating performance of the plant or facility *as designed* – and not as it may be at some time in the future, after spending money on improvements. In any event, an audit of a sample of the usual suspects listed below is generally worthwhile. The audit should include an examination of the basis for the scoping decision, which will be addressed in Chapter 4.

Some Important Operating Costs Affected by Project (Capital) Cost
The items/issues on this list can lead to additional project expenditure with reduced operating cost, or to economies in project cost with increased operating cost.

- **Labour Costs of Operation**
    - Degree of automation.
    - Provision of staff housing.
    - Provision of staff welfare facilities (insurance, hospital, healthcare, school, recreational, transport, canteen, retirement funding).

- Pre-operational training of local staff to obviate the employment of expensive expatriate specialists.[3]

• **Maintenance Costs of Operation**
- Provision of maintenance facilities (workshops, cranes, tools, vehicles, etc.) as opposed to getting maintenance performed by a contractor who provides such items.
- Expenditure on corrosion prevention, and on corrosion and wear reduction devices, coatings and materials.
- Purchase of more robust but more expensive machinery.

• **Energy Efficiency**
- Provision of more energy-efficient machinery and power transmission.
- Installation of devices to convert waste heat or waste products into usable energy.
- Increase of pipeline diameters to reduce energy losses.
- Installation of power-factor correction devices.
- Increased thermal insulation.

• **Other Major Input Cost Reduction**
- Identify the other major operating cost components such as fuels and production materials, and enquire what may be done to reduce them.

• **Operational Efficiency**
- Purchase and development of software to assist the operation (including financial and administrative operation).
- Initial staff training and training facilities, including simulators.
- (Capitalised) provision of specialists and equipment vendor engineers to assist with start-up and training.

• **Procurement Efficiency**
- Purchase of capital equipment from more expensive vendors from whom spare parts are more readily and economically available or can be manufactured locally.

---

3   A decision sometimes taken after careful consideration of local politics. In certain countries, it may be wise to employ expatriates for all the top technical positions, rendering the facility potentially worthless following nationalisation and the withdrawal of expatriates. Such policies will not be advertised!

- – Purchase of capital equipment together with a substantial inventory of spare parts, or negotiating their future purchase as part of the project procurement process, when better prices can be leveraged.
- – Manufacturing one's own utilities (steam, gases, etc.) rather than importing them.
- **Completeness of All Items Required for Operation**
  - – I am reminded of the purchase of hugely expensive military jets without the requirement for full maintenance manuals. Needless to say, these manuals eventually cost a fortune.

These are typical items. Taken together they can easily increase the cost of a facility by over 20% above the minimum for a facility that is still operable but costs more to run.

Some Considerations of Quality

The specified quality requirements for the project may cover some of these issues, and overall should have a major influence on the operating costs, efficiency and availability of the facility supplied. That is, after all, their main objective.

To summarise: the 'scope' sets out the purpose, definition and quantities of the project; the 'quality' specifications qualify the scope by defining characteristics that are important in determining the productive usefulness, operational efficiency, operational availability, maintenance costs and useful life of the project works.

There is an inherent problem when specifying quality, for instance by specifying applicable standards of manufacture and construction: operational practice will also affect the outcome. There is a school of practice that maintains that quality specifications are liable to incur unnecessary cost (they can – we will return to this) and should be kept as brief as possible, mainly requiring 'fitness for purpose'. This is a gross over-simplification. How fit, for how long, at what operational and maintenance cost, and how will such performance parameters be assured?

There are sometimes efforts to rely on an extended warranty rather than a detailed quality specification, or to relax quality requirements provided that an extended warranty is provided. The logic of this approach is usually that the warranty provides what is really required – an assurance of adequate performance over an extended period – whereas a quality specification is an indirect and therefore less certain means of achieving this end. The author's experience is that reliance on extended warranties is often a form of self-delusion. The longer the period of warranty, the more easily that suppliers can claim that problems have been caused by operational abuse and poor maintenance. And that's what they do!

As noted above, specifications can be over-elaborate and cause project cost increases that are not justified in terms of subsequent discounted lifecycle costs. This can come about in a number of ways:

- The project engineering team may be too far removed from the reality of operation, and develop 'grand designs' that satisfy their own aspirations but not the real needs. Such practice is variously described as 'building monuments', 'gold plating', etc. Ignorance or satisfaction of ego takes precedence over economic sense.
- The engineers, especially if driven to achieve economies of engineering cost, may be inclined to specify conservative designs rather than more cost-effective designs that require more engineering effort in the form of research and analysis.
- There may be deliberate unethical practices by which restrictive specifications are created to favour a particular supplier, rather than to get the best value for money from the market as a whole. Such piracy is best combated by critical external appraisal of the cost-effectiveness of proposed specifications in a market context – if necessary, by getting review and comment on draft specifications by the potential suppliers, before competitive tenders are issued.

Clearly, specification is of the essence of what is delivered as 'the project'. If specifications can be unilaterally relaxed by the Project Manager or Executive as the authorised project evolves, the possibility arises for the project pirate to make project savings at the expense of future operating costs. In short, to cook the project-performance books.

So how do we ensure that specifications are sufficient to deliver an optimum balance between project costs and future operating costs and revenues, but no more elaborate than necessary? And how do we ensure that any specification changes made during project execution are justified and balanced? Generally speaking, within any sort of organisation or macro-economic entity, an optimum outcome tends to be created if there is a fair balance of opposing interests. It is not realistic to expect the Director to be a part of the day-to-day process of achieving this balance; it is rather his role to ensure that the organisational set-up is designed to achieve such a balance, and to confirm this by an independent audit process.

The Director's overview role need not be too onerous or complex. In many instances – both corporate and government – it may be easily found that the mechanisms of balance are obviously inadequate (usually because of the dominance of a single interested party) and that the project's audit processes are superficial, e.g. restricted to financial examination rather than the essence of what is delivered.

A Typical Organisational Dynamic: Project versus Operations

In a typical poorly organised corporation or government department, there is a single entity responsible for structuring projects, setting performance targets, measuring project achievement and handing over the completed project to others for subsequent operation and use. This is, of course, a pirate's dream.

The most usual dynamic to avoid abuse is to create a constructively critical equilibrium between the project Executive and the entity charged with receiving and operating the project works (the Operator). Even if all the responsibilities within the project accountability train[4] are combined under one Executive, there can still be adequate balance as long as the Operator is truly independent of the Executive and gets adequate and timely information. There can be adequate balance, but there may not be!

- Especially in an old-established and hierarchical organisation, there can be collusion between the supposedly critically interactive parties, contrary to the overall interests of the enterprise as a whole (e.g. a relaxation of project specification in exchange for a private bar in a future executive office!).

---

4   The project accountability and incentive structure; see Chapter 1

- Or there can be destructive interaction, each party being too concerned with scoring points off the other.

If the organisation is large enough to afford it, a third party charged with oversight audit and referee functions is required.

4. Evaluating Business Plans

Standard Methodologies

From the foregoing, it should be appreciated that the only sound way to evaluate and manage the implementation of an economic project is by consideration of a long-term model, including a financial model. This must embrace everything that may affect or be affected by the project. The simplest and most usual form of model is the long-term financial spreadsheet, detailing monthly expenditure and revenue over the lifecycle of the project works. From the model, conclusions may be drawn in various formats.

'Economic' projects are meant to include any commercial or government project whose primary purpose is economic or welfare impact, and which can therefore be evaluated mainly (but not exclusively) in financial terms. Safety, security and environmental projects also require scrutiny, and may be found to be unjustified or ill conceived, often by quantitative means other than conventional financial analysis. These concerns will be addressed at the end of this chapter and in Chapter 17.

The fundamental need to compare the complete financial models that describe competing possible projects leads us immediately to a few economic analysis tools that are widely used in business economics. This book's focus is project piracy, not business economics as a whole, which indeed this author is not well qualified to present. The author is, however, (regrettably?) well qualified to present an overview of how the pirate may abuse business economics. We need to start with a brief outline of general business economic practices before proceeding (over several of the following chapters and the concluding summaries) to an examination of particular forms of abuse.

In order to compare competing financial models, the primary challenge is to reduce the model to a single figure. The monthly cost–revenue and cash flow totals are easily calculated by addition and subtraction; the question remains of how to meaningfully combine these monthly figures. This is conventionally done by discounting future cash flows to arrive at a single figure of NPV, or IRR, or attractiveness ratio. All these approaches have value and will therefore be briefly described. To support this presentation, a brief account of discounting practice, variations of its practical application and the derivation of simple mathematical formulae have been included as an Appendix.

Net Present Value

This is the most basic cash flow summation concept and is customarily defined as the following series (Equation 1):

$$NPV = (R_0 - C_0) + \frac{(R_1 - C_1)}{(1+d)} + \frac{(R_2 - C_2)}{(1+d)^2} + \dots + \frac{(R_{n-1} - C_{n-1})}{(1+d)^{n-1}}$$

where:
R_x is the revenue (or gross income) in year (or month) x,
C_x is the cost (investment or operating cost) in year (or month) x
d is the annual (or monthly) discount rate on future costs or revenue
n years (or months) is the period between project initiation and the final de-commissioning, the point at which costs and revenues cease

The resulting single-value roll-up can be used to compare projects or for comparison with no project at all, but its use has limitations. A project with negative NPV is clearly not economically worthwhile, while a project that has only a small NPV, but ties up a lot of investment and resources, is not very attractive. It is not enough to compare the NPV of competing projects; the NPV has to be considered in relation to the initial investment, which is best presented as the (negative) NPV excluding entries after cash flow becomes positive, defined as NPV_0 (changing the sign to make its value positive). The comparison of project value in relation to investment can be made in two ways: by calculating the IRR or the attractiveness ratio.

Internal Rate of Return
Referring to Equation 1, for a given series of revenues R_x and costs C_x, this is the value of discount factor for which the NPV is zero. It has to be calculated by convergence of successive approximations, possibly with the help of a suitably formulated spreadsheet. It is the most commonly used tool for comparing the relative attractiveness of projects in relation to the capital invested.

Attractiveness Ratio
This approach compares the expected NPV with the capital outlay, and is widely used in an informal fashion. However, it doesn't seem to have any standard presentation or definition, recognised by academic economists or financial analysts. The problem with making this comparison informally is that informal usage leads to vagueness of targets and hence abuse. Let's define the attractiveness ratio as NPV/NPV_0. This gives a good idea of the relative attractiveness of a potential investment with respect to a limited availability of capital or limited capacity to carry out projects. It can be determined directly without iteration.

All projects carry risks of various kinds, which will be considered in more detail later. The maximum risk for an investor in a limited company is the value of the investment, NPV_0; the expected reward is the NPV. Thus the attractiveness ratio is an inverse indication of risk/reward potential.

This analysis allows for a useful split between shareholders' capital and debt. For the purpose under discussion, it is permissible to deduct the value of debt when calculating NPV_0, but include the repayment of debt and interest as a cost in the NPV calculation, giving a simple comparative indicator of the value of the geared entity in relation to shareholders' investment.

NPV Uncertainties and Manipulations
All three of these tools have NPV evaluation as their fundamental basis. Consider the spreadsheet used to calculate the NPV: it is made up of

an array of itemised costs to be incurred and revenues to be received in the future. Few of these cost or revenue entries have a certain value. Some of the associated items are much more accurately predictable than others, but all reflect a degree of assumption about the future. To gauge how realistically the NPV has been calculated, there is no substitute for an experienced review of the projected monthly spreadsheet, broken down to show at least 20 separable groupings of capital and operating costs respectively. This review should include a 'what if?' analysis of the more significant items, and especially those highlighted by formal risk analysis.

Another important spreadsheet shows cash flow corresponding to the cost–revenue spreadsheet and the project funding. This incorporates the project funding from defined sources, and the corresponding out-flows or inflows of interest and dividend, including any taxes or other financial transactions not displayed in the cost–revenue spreadsheet (for whatever dubious reasons). This spreadsheet also requires risk analysis and 'what if?' testing.

These two spreadsheets are the essential financial definition of the project: not any one-line roll-up stating a single undiscounted cost esti-mate value, time to completion and annual operating revenue. Cost roll-ups that are suitably discounted to yield present values are useful for comparative purposes and to focus on the real project target of NPV, but over-reliance even on these is questionable (as will be addressed later). It seems to be glaringly obvious that summarising capital costs, without time-based discounting or allowing for interest earned on unexpended cash, should only be used to convey an order-of-magnitude idea of the project. As a control, an undiscounted cost is much too vague, except for relatively simple and quickly completed projects. For major and com-plex projects, to accept these values as overall targets creates spaces within which pirates can operate, just as a smart financial programmer can take a fraction of a cent off each bank transaction and make a for-tune. And yet this practice is widespread, perhaps not internally, but at least in the disclosure of project performance reports. I wonder why?

Behind each figure in the spreadsheet presented for project authori-sation, there should be available a back-up of information about how the figure was derived; an audit trail, in fact, going back to the documented design and costing of the items in question. No major project should be authorised without adequate testing of this audit trail by checking its completeness and accuracy, thus ensuring that individual trails do not end at guessed or factorised costs for items defined too vaguely to permit subsequent evaluation of their delivery. Particular attention ought to be paid to issues which lead to a trade-off between capital and operating costs, as listed in Chapter 3.

Subsequent chapters include discussion of more project study aspects that should be scrutinised. For the present, a little more on simple financial analysis tools.

Trade-off Analysis

Usually the purpose defining a project can be served in many different ways. There are different possible configurations of the project components, including in particular those which affect post-project performance and operating costs, as considered previously. Trade-off analysis is the process of optimising the project configuration according to enterprise performance criteria. Trade-off analysis requires long-term performance comparison between different possible models. The simplest way to go about this is to start with a base model and explore the effects of changing it. The most obvious and complete way to examine a possible change to the project (maybe to more than one component at a time) is by testing the effect of making the corresponding changes to the computerised spreadsheets. This is not always possible and is not always recommended.

- The electronic spreadsheets may not be readily available to the Director. They may be the property of a third-party consultant or contractor.
- The available versions, often derived as a series of interlinked spreadsheets each containing hundreds of interlinking formulae, may be unnecessarily complex for a simple 'what if?' task. It is a widespread issue that, wonderful as computerised spreadsheets can be as number-crunching devices, they also lead to errors. These include major errors that would be unlikely in a non-computerised process. Although the spreadsheet format is ideal for displaying cost–time relationships, many project practitioners forbid reliance on computer spreadsheets to summate costs.

The use of computers unfortunately can bypass the individual judgement of common sense which is exercised over each information input and arithmetical operation done manually.

There is still room to use quick-judgement formulae, as were used before computers became widely available.

The simplest formula is to consider only a single lump-sum capital expenditure T, to be spent on an additional project feature (or reconfiguration) that will result in a regular flow of future savings (or additional income) S. We wish to establish the discounted 'present value' P of these savings to compare with the value of T. Equation 1 can be simplified and summed to yield Equation 2:

$$P = S \times \frac{1 - D^n}{1 - D} \qquad \text{(Equation 2)}$$

where:

P is the present value of the feature

S is the saving (or benefit) derived in one unit of time (years or months)

n is the number of years (or months) over which the feature will be effective

D is the annual (or monthly) discount factor

Notes:

1. D is defined as the annual or monthly ratio of future value to present value, and corresponds to $1/(1 + d)$ in the formula for NPV presented above. The discount rate d is an important value to be decided on and understood for any project. It is primarily an 'internal' rate for the project Owner, internal because it corresponds to the rates of interest available and to the 'opportunity cost' of money to that specific Owner at that specific time. It cannot be calculated from a universally-applicable formula, it is rather an instrument of policy.

2. This formula is here presented in its simplest form, I do not wish to burden this text with further detail. Refer to the Appendix for the derivation of the formula, and several possible refinements to increase accuracy in certain circumstances, together with further

discussion of discounting practice. Anyone wishing to apply this methodology in practice should first consult the Appendix.

P/S is a dimensionless ratio. Having established its value for the project, it is easily used as a 'pay-off' period (in years or months) to decide whether each proposed operational cost-saving feature is justified. This procedure is mathematically exactly equivalent to the NPV assessment: a 'pay-off period' of x years, when calculated thus, exactly corresponds to an NPV of zero for a project or project feature for which P/S is equal to x.

Note that a 'pay-off' period calculated in this way does *not* imply that after period x the investment has been completely repaid. It has not. The interest or cost-of-money has not yet been repaid.

For example, if we are addressing a potential feature that will operate over the 20-year life of the investment ($n = 20$ years) and the annualised discount rate d is 10%, then

$$D = 1/(1 + d) = 1/1.1 = .91$$
$$\frac{P}{S} = \frac{1 - .91^{20}}{1 - .91} = 9.4 \text{ years}$$

The cost of the feature has to be no more than 9.4 times the value of the annual savings (net of any additional maintenance costs incurred) for the feature to be economically justified. Put another way, if the feature has this P/S ratio, the investment yields an NPV of zero, and any actual P/S ratio above this upper-limit value is uneconomical. The Appendix examines ways to use IRR and attractiveness ratio criteria to decide on a lower-limit value of P/S below which incorporation of the feature is definitely recommended.

Well, that's the mathematically correct way of performing the 'trade-off' analysis, but it's one thing to be mathematically correct, and another to be practically realistic.

- The discount rate is in practice a very difficult quantity to determine, dealing as it does with expectations of future finance availability. The discount rate at which a corporation or even a government has to operate can change very quickly as adverse or cash-rich circumstances arise. If no further finance or debt is available at all, it may effectively become infinite: no further expenditure can be justified, whatever the benefit.

- There is always a risk that the additional investment will not be as effective as expected. (It seldom turns out to be more effective.) For instance, if a supplier of machinery knows that additional claimed efficiency will justify a higher price, the critical appraiser should anticipate that he may lie about the efficiency just about as much as he thinks he can get away with. This might be quite a considerable margin if the efficiency is hard and expensive to measure accurately in a practical situation.

These considerations do *not* mean that investing more to save money later is not justifiable. Such arguments will inevitably be used by the pirate attempting to gloss over a capital expenditure economy at the cost of eventual extra operating expense. Ultimately, any investment can only be justified in terms of the results achieved, which means operating profit, which is directly decreased by any operating cost increase. And, as previously noted, installing operating expense reduction features later is liable to cost far more than incorporating them at the outset.

Considerations of uncertainty do however create a need to supplement the decision-making process by exercising practical judgement as outlined in the following. Wherever applicable, reduce the projected operational cost savings by a calculated amount that compensates for the frequent possibility that some of the savings will not in fact materialise. My usual recommendation is that this reduction should include an amount corresponding to the 'testing tolerances' for verification of the savings and for normal operational deterioration. For instance, if it's unlikely to be possible to measure the efficiency of a proposed power-consuming (or power-saving or -generating) device to closer than 4%, take 4% off the quoted efficiency when performing this analysis. If in its average operational condition the efficiency is liable to deteriorate by a further 3%, take that off as well.

As a more general qualification of the analysis, it should be noted that we have tacitly assumed that a proposed change does not alter the risk profile of the project or of subsequent operation. This possibility has to be considered, and if found to be the case, appropriate adjustment to the calculated present value must be made (up or down). The adjustment can be made as per the practice recommended in the preceding paragraph for possible non-delivery of expected efficiency (which I have cynically implied to mean likely non-delivery), or by quantified risk analysis (to be addressed later).

Failure to optimise on future energy costs is probably one of the false economies most widely practised by project pirates. Energy cost savings seem to be destined to become increasingly more important. For any project involving the use or generation of significant electrical power, the present value of an extra kilowatt consumed or generated should be calculated and used as a major design and performance criterion.

For instance, given a proposal to build a plant with a 25-year life, if 1 kWh of electricity costs $0.05 (US) and the discount rate d is 10%, the present value P of an extra kilowatt saved or generated is given by:

$$D = 1/(1 + d) = 1/1.1 = .91$$
$$\frac{P}{S} = \frac{1 - .91^{25}}{1 - .91} = 10 \text{ years}$$

Assuming the plant operates for 90% of the hours in a year,

$$P = 90\% \times 365 \times 24 \times 10 \times \$0.05 = \$3940/kW$$

This is usually such an important figure that it should be calculated not with this simple formula, but on a detailed spreadsheet, taking into account all that is known about future likely cost increases. Usually, it is worthwhile to spend considerable extra investment to reduce power costs. And it's not good enough just to specify, design and attempt to purchase power-saving features. The costs involved are usually high enough to warrant extra project expenditure on inspection and testing, to ensure that the power savings actually materialise.

When considering the performance of an entire plant that consumes significant power, it is surely inconceivable that the performance criteria should not include power consumption, verified by stringent performance testing. There should be a meaningful penalty or bonus for power efficiency, to drive the inclusion of appropriate power-saving features.

If the plant consumes a lot of expensive fuel or other commodity, the same arguments apply. Look at the operational cost–time spreadsheet and address all the expensive operational items in the same way.

Cost and Revenue Inflation

Because different practices are involved in addressing future cost inflation, this subject has largely been avoided. But it is far too important to be ignored.

I once worked for a large oil company in which the usual practice when addressing project economics was to ignore inflation completely, on the basis that increases in cost would be countered by increases in revenue. That was 40 years ago. I doubt that they're still doing the same thing, but some other firms still are. I'm not sure that the underlying reason isn't simply laziness, or a disinclination to address something that is inherently uncertain. Some of the relevant management issues will be discussed in future chapters. Here I will simply note the economic evaluation aspects of the treatment of inflation which should always be included, and then state my personal views on what else should be done. There are libraries of economic theory on this subject – this may be taken as an indication of the underlying uncertainties, but that should be no excuse for ignoring the effects.

The general requirement is that assumptions about the treatment and prediction of inflation be clearly set out in the proposed project's financial review, along with the calculation of how the economic evaluations would be correspondingly modified. It may be that different inflationary scenarios will be assumed, and calculations made on a 'what if?' basis for each scenario, leaving the final decision to the investor. This is good practice for project evaluation, and a necessary part of risk evaluation; following such analysis, risk management plans may also be developed to mitigate unacceptable scenarios. But it's impractical to use a number of scenarios as the project control base. Multiple alternative targets will cause extreme confusion, besides creating space for pirates to operate. There must be a project baseline case for the treatment of inflation. The question remains of how to choose this.

My personal opinion is that to use a baseline case that ignores inflation is an invitation for sub-optimal management (a point to be developed further in Chapter 11). There are at least two major objections to the practice of excluding inflation from economic evaluation on the basis that cost changes are likely to be countered by revenue increases:

- It can surely never be wise to ignore whatever knowledge may be available to reach an informed prediction of events, and instead to fall back on a catch-all formula.
- Any assumptions about inflation from costs and revenues having been removed, the same treatment needs to be applied to the discount rate. The discount rate, like prevailing interest rates, always reflects some degree of assumption about future inflation, and it is very difficult if not impossible to pinpoint this. To take inflationary effects out of cost and revenue but not the discount rate is fallacious.

A fundamental underlying issue is that, in making economic comparisons, the starting point is that we should compare alternative complete models of a business, in other words the complete time-based spreadsheets previously discussed. The complete models need to be as close as we can get to the reality of what will actually happen in the future. For reality, the models must include both the expected future inflation and the actual cost of money in accordance with a finance plan. The cost of money will often incorporate a market assessment of the project risk, unless full collateral is employed.

NPV or IRR analysis has to be practised in the light that these are just tools for trying to reduce the complexity of the model to a single figure for comparative purposes. The same applies to the chosen discount rate; it is an over-simplification of reality, useful as a tool but only in so far as its use provides a meaningful reflection of the underlying business complexity.

Different phenomena, for instance the declining availability of fossil fuels and of land, affect the inflation of project cost and revenue components in different ways. For a large project, it should be worthwhile to consider the inflation of each major cost or revenue component separately. By 'consider' I mean evaluate at the pre-project stage, not necessarily incorporating different inflationary values for each component in the spreadsheet, unless significant differences are seen. Simplicity is also desirable, provided that it does not mask significant issues.

In conclusion, I recommend that:

a. Project economic justification and the decision whether to proceed with the project should consider a range of inflationary scenarios, just as for any other important uncertain parameter.

b. The project target, the control base spreadsheets and the capital–operating-cost trade-off analyses should be based on well-informed forecasts of future costs at the escalated values which will actually be incurred. The same treatment should be applied to revenues and interest rates.

c. The discount rate used for NPV evaluation should be a simple evaluation of the opportunity cost of money at the time that it is required.

The inflationary factors decided upon and the underlying assumptions should be clearly stated as part of the project's financial definition. The same applies to the cost of finance. If there are significant changes to the actual or predicted factors or to the underlying assumptions as the project progresses, they should trigger revised analysis and management action just as for any other deviation from the control-base target as was outlined in relation to cost and time. More on this follows in subsequent chapters.

Whenever project performance criteria and measurements are based on single-line roll-ups, without ultimate reference to the complete time-based model, opportunities are created for manipulation. And that's what happens when a reality such as inflation is ignored.

Non-economic Projects

There are many types of project for which economic and financial justification don't readily apply, often because the project objectives are essentially spiritual or social, such as building a cathedral or a cultural facility. However, there are also many types of project which may not be advocated or analysed on economic grounds, but which can in fact be subjected to financial or other quantitative analysis although their protagonists don't attempt this. This may arise from ignorance, in the belief that the need for the project is 'self-evident', but there may also be a deliberate strategy of emotional manipulation in support of a project that might not survive dispassionate scrutiny. Remember that financial analysis, or the attempt to break down issues into financial terms, is not advocated even for economic projects as the only important analysis. But it is a very useful form of analysis and where possible should never be overlooked.

Projects intended to enhance safety and security fall under the umbrella of 'risk analysis and management'. Using techniques that will be briefly addressed later, it is often possible to examine a project's justification in financial terms. This may raise objections of the type 'How can you put a price on human life and suffering?' The answer to this is that the analysis does not put a price on the certainty that any particular individual will become a casualty– this is never permissible – but instead assesses the *probability* of an accident occurring because of a hazard that is known and accepted by the individuals involved, and comparison of this probability with risks commonly accepted, such as travel by various means. This has to do with the prioritisation of limited resources, an objective that would not be achieved in a '100% safe' environment in which everyone stays in bed and ultimately we all starve to death[5].

Projects for environmental protection are often motivated by quality-of-life or spiritual objectives which are not easily expressed in cash terms, but they still require cash for their implementation, which entails that less cash is available for competing objectives. It is still necessary to compare what will be achieved with what will be sacrificed elsewhere to reach a balanced decision. Especially because the project outcome may not be expressed in financial terms, it is essential to ensure that the apparent benefits are worthwhile when viewed in a broader context. An attempt is made to illustrate this in Chapter 17.

---

5   This practice is usually known as Hazan, and is outlined in the works of Trevor Kletz. Refer to Amazon or similar sites for his relevant publications.

5. Project Estimating

Estimating Basics

An estimate is one of the most fundamental and essential project management tools. Without it, there can be no informed project authorisation and no meaningful cost control. In order to address some important issues arising from estimate manipulation, it is necessary to start with some basics.

We are dealing with major projects, not the estimating of costs for repeated or routine operations, which is comparatively easy. However, most projects are not completely original; previous projects have been carried out with a greater or lesser degree of similarity. From the historic data available, it is often possible to extrapolate (or interpolate) a project cost expectation. The accuracy will depend mainly on the degree of similarity between the present and past projects in every aspect – project definition and physical description, location, labour practices, timing, etc. 'Accuracy' is here used loosely, as per customary practice. What is strictly meant is 'confidence of being correct', which is a bit of a mouthful. Thus 'accuracy of +/–30%' means a high level of confidence that the eventual cost will lie within these bounds. A discussion of this follows later.

The accuracy of an extrapolated estimate also depends on the skills and database of the estimator, but it is unlikely to be considered to be more accurate than +/–15% when there is close similarity to the base used for comparison. Often it is much less, e.g. +/–30%.

To produce an estimate that considers all the special needs and circumstances of a particular project, and is usable as a basis for project control, requires that all the significant aspects of the proposed project, and factors that may affect them, are understood in their entirety. There must be little room for surprise problems to emerge at the project execution stage. Thus 'estimating' skills are usually just the final part of getting an accurate estimate. Without adequate up-front investigations and engineering of aspects of the project which are different from previous documented experience, accuracy is not possible. In the following, we begin by assuming that all the investigations and engineering have been completed to produce a workable and sufficiently detailed conceptual design. As outlined in previous chapters, the designs used for estimating also have to consider all significant aspects of operation after the project has been completed. Otherwise there is no way that the required project expectations can be assured over the longer term.

There are certain types of large project, and certain project circumstances, in which it is found possible to completely design the project works and the operational practices before estimating the project cost. These are very much the exception, for large projects, because usually the costs that have to be incurred and the time delay before authorisation are unacceptable. Pre-project estimates have to be based on a conceptual design, and considerable skill and experience are required (more so in more complex projects) to ensure that this design arrives at parameters that will end up costing the same and performing the same as the final detailed design.

There are four main ingredients of an estimate which we need to address here: list of components or parts, estimate of quantities, estimate of 'direct' costs (component direct cost = quantity × price) and estimate of 'indirect' costs. Following this, we will address the accuracy of the estimate, and how costs may be controlled using the estimate as a base – which will enable us to see some opportunities for pirates.

Estimate of Parts and Quantities
In order to produce a pre-project estimate, experienced engineers and estimators have various tricks and short cuts by which they may

concentrate on the more important aspects of a 'conceptual' design. They focus attention on those aspects which are different from previous designs, and use as much applicable data from previous experience as they can. But, in general, a complete (usually, preliminary) design and a corresponding 'bill of quantities' must be produced. These may then be used, in conjunction with appropriate specifications, firstly for estimating project costs – usually by soliciting prices ('bids') from the market – and subsequently as a control base for the approved project.

It is customary to break this list down into two parts: 'direct field cost' (DFC) items and 'indirect field cost' (IFC) items. The DFC items are essentially material objects, such as structures, that become part of the final physical project delivery; the corresponding prices include the costs of their purchase, delivery to the project site, construction and commissioning. DFC costs are traditionally broken down according to the engineering discipline or specialist responsible for their design or management, e.g. civil, mechanical, structural, electrical, instrumentation, piping, transport, construction, operation, maintenance, product marketing. Each specialist produces a list of requirements and their quantities and pricing, possibly with the assistance of professional quantity surveyors, estimators and procurement specialists. The specialist can then be held accountable at the project stage for working within the bounds of the estimate.

Prices and Their Uncertainty

If the designs (including all 'soft' aspects of design such as project and operational planning, financial planning, future operating methodology, etc.) have been well thought out, and accurate corresponding bills of quantities are available, the cost estimate can still be no more accurate than the accuracy of the forecast prices for the goods and services required.

Self-deception about the accuracy of prices, or deception of others (often unwittingly), may result from placing too much reliance on actual pre-project 'bids' received from suppliers and contractors. These bids are unlikely to be binding – even if quoted as being 'valid for x months' – because of a number of circumstances:

- The specifications/designs/quantities issued for pre-project pricing will change or be modified at the project stage. They usually become more detailed as final designs replace conceptual or preliminary designs.
- New and more detailed commercial conditions of contract will be wanted at the project stage.
- Some of the project circumstances, and in particular the time schedule, will have changed.
- The bid validity period, for what it is worth, will have expired.
- The manager of the eventual project will want to solicit new competitive bids anyway at the project stage – hoping for better offers – and will hardly be able, even morally, to hold first-time-around bidders to their previous offers under such circumstances.
- The bid prices are subject to adjustment according to many secondary circumstances, e.g. labour rates, commodity prices, foreign exchange rate changes, published cost indices, 'demand inflation' (whatever that may be taken to mean).

When incorporating these bids into the estimate, estimators have to make judgements that amount to forecasting the future. They may for instance be concerned that bidders offered lower prices than may be available at the project stage, in order to appear competitive and knowing that no order could result at the present stage. It is more usual, on the other hand, to believe that prices may be too high – for the same reason! It's guesswork; the bidders won't tell you, or can't be trusted if they do. For many of the more significant parts of a big project, such as major construction works or custom-built machinery, it requires a lot of expensive work on the part of the bidders to come up with an accurate project-specific price. Does anybody really expect them to do that meticulously, when the purchaser will almost certainly reissue bid requests in the event of a project? If there is eventually a project.

On the subject of self-delusion, I have come across senior executives, in project-contracting companies, who say to their estimating teams when preparing a tender for a project, 'Let's get really competitive prices from our prospective sub-contractors so that we in turn will be really competitive.' I'm serious: senior executives who were that deluded. When at the eventual project stage, for whatever purported reasons, the sub-contractors' prices were much higher, they blamed the Project Manager!

Another form of self-delusion is to use firm prices that have to be put forward by an 'in-house' service organisation. For instance, an Army Corps of Engineers may base a project estimate on prices from their own Construction Arm, which doesn't have the luxury of chang-ing the prices at a later stage. All this does is shift risk from the Project Arm (whose estimators may therefore pride themselves on their record of accuracy) to another part of the organisation. No net gain in certainty. No need to be concerned about the Construction Arm either: doing in-house work, they will make up for the risk by inflating their prices, or by effectively subsidising their prices by using infrastructure already paid for by the taxpayer.

The Owner of the prospective project can try to get around these issues of uncertainty by making a pre-project 'partnership' deal with pro-spective suppliers and contractors. Such deals are liable to be severely abused and are seldom good value to the Owner. Better to let competi-tion take its course and live with some uncertainty of future cost, rather than the certainty of being ripped off by a 'project partner'. Sometimes, ripped off with benefits of 'partnership' flowing in devious ways to the Owner's own project Executives (some examples will be given later).

In conclusion, there is always uncertainty about future costs. There are many factors, market forces in particular, that reduce the certainty of cost forecasts of future business deals in inverse proportion to the size, complexity and timescale of a project. It is possible to remove some uncertainty, but only at an extra cost that is likely to push the total cost up to the top end of the range of uncertainty anyway. This practice is seldom compatible with getting best value.

Indirect Field Costs

This is a grouping of project costs for items that are not physically delivered to and constructed into the project works, such as the costs of project management and engineering, office overheads, insurance, banking and finance charges, and the like. Note:

Total cost = DFC + IFC

Having calculated the IFC by estimating the cost of its components, it is common practice to express IFC as a percentage of total cost or of DFC, for comparison with previous experience. The major portion of the IFC is usually the cost of engineering and project management (E&M), and it is not unusual for inexperienced Directors to get the idea that a low IFC (or E&M) percentage is evidence of E&M efficiency, and the reverse if the percentage is high.

DFC/IFC Piracy

Note that the differentiation of costs between DFC and IFC (or E&M costs) is not based on any absolute unwavering definition, and can be quite fluid, depending on the project approach adopted. Here are some examples of different project execution methods that have a major effect on apparent IFC or E&M costs:

1. The project is managed by a consultant who prepares a specification for the entire project works to be delivered on a 'turnkey basis'. All the project design and management activities (other than the conceptual work required for the contract specification) are performed by the contractor and are included (without separate breakdown) in the turnkey price, which is reported as the DFC. Only the consultant's cost plus a few sundries are reported as IFC, which amounts to typically 3–4% of the DFC.

2. A Managing Contractor is appointed to carry out the project on a 'reimbursable' basis. He is paid according to man-hours expended and makes most of his money out of the mark-up on man-hour rates. He therefore does the maximum of engineering work himself, and also breaks down the procurement work into a large number of packages, thus maximising the amount of management man-hours. Note that no extra work is necessarily created overall; most of the work is performed by a different party than in case 1 and thus is reported differently in the project accounts. In this case, the reported IFC may be as much as 20% of the DFC.

3. The Managing Contractor does rather little engineering and design work himself, maybe because he is paid a fixed fee. He breaks the procurement up into a small number of large design-and-build contracts, i.e. packages that include much of the engineering and design work. With few procured packages,

the management costs are also greatly reduced. Compared with case 2, there will be large savings on reported IFC. But the same amount of E&M work still has to be done overall. The reported DFC will be inflated accordingly.

There are often equally valid alternative project execution methodologies, and the project's particular circumstances are likely to dictate the preferred choice. For instance, method 2 above lends itself to rapid project execution, with much of the engineering design, manufacture and construction work being carried out in parallel. Method 1 is often preferred where more time is available to get the best contracting deals and contain costs, if the project timescale permits that. Method 3 may be used as a compromise between these circumstances, or when some critical aspects of project performance require more of the Owner's attention than others.

Directors should be careful about any claims about what should be the 'right' E&M costs for a project. It is easy to cook the books, and comparisons made between different projects are often invalid. The only reasonably reliable way to appraise proposed or historic projects is an in-depth expert review of the methodology and work breakdown for the whole project.

Executive Influence

Given the many estimating uncertainties, it is often rather easy for a forceful Executive to get even a competent and professional team of engineers and estimators to shift the cost estimate in the direction he wants. Consider these remarks:

'Is this really the best you can come up with? How do you think we can compete in such pedestrian fashion? Don't you people care about the future of the business?'

'Are we quite sure we can achieve this? Another project like XYZ will ruin us.'

In semi-serious vein, one very experienced contracting professional used to define a cost estimate as being the value that the CEO required, and estimating as the process of arriving at this figure.

This Executive influence is often not a manifestation of piracy at all. It may be the most valuable business process of the enterprise, when targets are set at the challenging end of a range of uncertainty. On the other hand, such influence may be exercised with piratical intent, depending on who stands to gain or lose, in the long term. For the Owner, the main issue is to understand and approve the intent. Are we dealing with a driving CEO who is setting tough targets that he will get his team to achieve? Or is this a pedestrian CEO who is content to let the business decay as he goes on pension? Or is this CEO an opportunist who has seen an avenue for short-term personal gain at long-term corporate expense? Is his money where his mouth is?

In practice these are not easy questions to answer until project implementation is well advanced and a historical view can be taken. But with really experienced oversight and a good knowledge of the organisation in question, it should be possible to know the answers at the time of approval of the project target. Further chapters will address some of the underlying issues.

Unachievable Targets

When reviewing project estimates, it is useful to look at the pre-project process by which cost and time estimates were set. If there is a history of downward movement of successive estimates, look very carefully at the justification for the change, the actual improvements of design or any better component prices on offer. If downward movement is found to be arising only out of differing 'views' being taken of the same information, influenced possibly by 'pressure from the top', enquire whether possible upward movement received the same attention.

6. Risk Evaluation and Management

Risk and Directors' Responsibilities

We considered above some of the project cost-estimating risks, including the risk arising from design development from the pre-project stage (used for project cost estimating) to the final project designs. This risk can only be controlled by the project engineers and designers, who must be held accountable that the final designs do not become more elaborate or expensive. We also considered some of the basic pricing risks. Of course, there are invariably very many more risks, including:

- Major unpredictable events such as social unrest, riots, war, weather catastrophes and strikes: these are classified as force majeure and will be addressed later.
- Monetary inflation and exchange rate variation. These issues are sometimes 'qualified out' from estimates (and from the project manager's accountability!), a dubious practice that will also be addressed later.
- Aside from general monetary inflation, there are often specialised aspects of demand inflation that come about in relation to specific commodities and skills. These can impact on the project in two main ways: by increasing the cost of scarce resources, and by causing sub-standard project performance when key resources are insufficiently available. It is not easy to

measure such phenomena; these are risks that have to be identified and managed.

- And then there are just plain incidents: ships that sink, trucks that crash and acts of theft. Matters like accident and theft will usually be covered by insurance, but there is usually a 'knock-on' or 'consequential' effect that cannot readily be covered by insurance or penalty. A unique item may be lost at sea and the insurers will pay for the replacement but not the cost of rectifying the overall construction schedule or the cost of late completion.

- Sub-surface surprises: foundations that need to go far deeper than was reasonably expected; mines that turn out not to be economically mineable. Geo-technical engineering and mine planning have in common that it is not economically viable to perform enough sub-surface investigation to be 100% certain of what may be encountered at the project stage.

- Harmfully aggressive government authorities.

- Incompetence: managers, suppliers and contractors who underperform. The suppliers' and contractors' direct non-performance should be covered by contract penalties, but once again the knock-on effects can seldom be covered. The possible need to change suppliers and contractors in mid-project can be extremely damaging to both project cost and schedule.

- Technology risks. These can be very severe when new ('bleeding-edge') technology is involved, but can also exist in a more subtle fashion, such as when the special circumstances of the project were insufficiently understood. For instance, an ore or feedstock composition may differ from expectations, resulting in the chosen processing technology becoming inadequate. Alternative technology development may make the technology employed in the project obsolescent and uncompetitive, especially in rapidly developing fields such as computers and their applications.

- Engineering and project implementation risks. These may be considered a combined subset of incompetence and technology risks. 'What can go wrong' spans a vast compendium of possibilities, many of which have led to past disasters. 'Incompetence' has to be seen in context here: although simple negligence or lack of necessary knowledge or skills may be the cause of fail-ure, 'poor judgement', possibly of a highly professional kind, may retrospectively be considered responsible, especially in applications of complex, advanced and novel technology.

Risk management has always been one of the central tasks of man-aging anything. If we define a risk as an uncertainty, then that's all that can be managed; the certainties will take care of themselves! Many of the professions involved in project management have in recent years been highly involved in codifying risk management techniques, and a plethora of consultants are usually available to offer their services. National and international (ISO) standards have evolved. With this cod-ification has come an attempt to standardise vocabulary. Whereas in the past project risk was usually regarded as any uncertainty that could affect the outcome of the project, the codified definition is generally that Risk is a quantity, the product of the probability of an event happening multiplied by the estimated impact of the event if it happens. This can usually be expressed as a cash amount. Many risks such as pricing risks can have an upside as well as a downside. This quantified expression of risk will be referred to as 'Risk' in what follows.

In order to describe some of the failings and abuses associated with risk management, it is necessary first to provide a brief overview of a process which the Director should require to be exercised in far more detail by competent professionals. As a reminder of the Director's prime responsibilities, the following was extracted verbatim from the 2002 report published by the (UK) Institute of Risk Management, the Association of Insurance and Risk Managers and the National Forum for Risk Management in the Public Sector. The full report is freely available on the internet.

'The Board of Directors should:
- know about the most significant risks facing the organisation
- know the possible effects on shareholder value of deviations to expected performance ranges
- ensure appropriate levels of awareness throughout the organisation
- know how the organisation will manage a crisis

know the importance of stakeholder confidence in the organisation

know how to manage communications with the investment community where applicable

- be assured that the risk management process is working effectively
- publish a clear risk management policy covering risk management philosophy and responsibilities.'

In the context of the authorisation of a large and important project, and with particular reference to the penultimate responsibility, let us briefly address the question of how the Director should 'be assured'. This is the nub of the present issue of preventing piracy associated with excessive risk.

In the first place, this should be by personal review of a comprehensive project risk analysis and management report, with the following in mind:

- The report should contain a concise executive summary, listing the outcome of the processes outlined below, namely
  (1) the most important identified risks,
  (2) the probabilities of their occurrence,
  (3) the assessed impacts if they do occur,
  (4) the mitigation requirements, and
  (5) a summary of residual Risks (after mitigation) with the corresponding management plans.

The bulk of the report should be presented for reference only, in case of need for verification or further explanation. If the executive summary is inadequate or vague, bin the report and demand something that is both concise and includes commitment to clear recommendations.

- The report should correspond to a quoted revision of the project charter document (to be discussed later).
- The report should be used as a 'live' document for the duration of the project, and should be reviewed periodically and when any major changes are contemplated or major incidents occur.

- A basic 'overview checklist' will be presented, following a brief summary of the basic risk management process (at the management rather than technical level).

Risk Management Basics

The basic processes of risk analysis are:

Identify.
Evaluate.
Mitigate.

Following these processes, risk management decisions are taken on how to reformat and proceed with the project and how to follow up on identified concerns.

Risk identification must be carried out by people who are knowledgeable in the appropriate (usually technical) field, usually employing a checklist based on previous experience. These experts have to be thoroughly acquainted with the project being reviewed, and thus the participation of the project team leaders is normally considered essential. The project members who performed and will perform the work have a critical responsibility to expose any doubts or shortcomings. All assumptions and known uncertainties must be exposed for review.

Note that all the risks can only be properly identified if the project has first been defined, as outlined in Chapter 2. Risk analysis of an inadequately defined project is inherently flawed. By the same token, if there is any change in the project definition, any previously performed risk analysis should be reconsidered and if necessary re-performed. At the technical level, any proposed change to a project or to an operating entity (especially in a hazardous environment) should in itself be regarded as a risk until proven otherwise by a suitably qualified person and process.

We are dealing with a whole host of possible projects here, and the risk identification methodology differs according to the type of project and its environment. As a general rule, the risk identification process can be divided into a few major parts:

- Evaluation of the completeness and quality of the work carried out to define, design and quantify the project; and, arising out of this (and after fixing any immediately fixable shortcomings), identifying perceived difficulties and uncertainties that may affect the project outcome. 'The work' being assessed here includes all the required designs and studies for safety and environmental impact, market studies, financial analysis – everything that the project may include or impact on.

- Processing a checklist of problems and difficulties known to have arisen in similar past projects and operations, including the system failures within which individual failures arose.
- Evaluation and identification of weaknesses in the proposed project execution methodology and resources, including the track record and motivation of the organisations and individuals to be involved and the quality assurance (QA) measures to be adopted.

Risks thus identified are evaluated by the assessment of the probability of occurrence and the consequential impact, thereby arriving at a quantified Risk.

There are many possible forms of risk mitigation; in particular:

- Redesign or reconfigure the project to avoid or reduce the Risk.
- Develop and require management, design, construction and operational practices to eliminate or reduce the Risk. These may include improved methods, oversight, inspection, checks and reports.
- Develop a better understanding of the risk, e.g. by getting more information or expert advice. This may result in a change to the evaluation of the Risk, or to redesign, or both.
- Pass part or all of the Risk onto others, by insurance or by agreement with other entities (project contractors, project clients or buyers of end products, investors, etc.).
- Abandon the project, or suspend it until better methodology is available.

Aside from abandoning the project completely, mitigation measures have to be optimised. Commercially, there is no point in spending more on mitigation than the value of the Risk, provided this has been accurately evaluated. The optimum for the project is the point at which any further mitigation cost exceeds the corresponding value of Risk reduction. Often this is found to be when the cost of the mitigating measures is similar to the assessed value of Risk remaining after mitigation.

Legally, certain risks may be simply inadmissible, whatever the value of assessed Risk, especially where human life or health is involved. If such risks are legally permissible – and they may well be, if the hazards apply only to specific groups of individuals, who are fully aware of them and are trained to deal with them – utilise Hazan analysis as discussed in Chapter 4.

The final pre-project task of the risk manager is to assemble a report, the contents of which were previously addressed. Note that various industries have their own highly developed technologies for risk management and in particular the management of potential hazards. Often, and increasingly, there is a regulatory body to oversee this, such as a nuclear energy regulator. For the project Owner, this entity may ease the safety concerns, but usually becomes the source of another major risk to the project, because such bodies are inclined to be slow and unresponsive to the needs of the project schedule and budget.

Independence
It is clearly in the Owner's interests to ensure that the risk analysis process is headed by a party that is independent of the project team and the Executive. Even a nominally independent party may be susceptible to being influenced in one way or another. A question to ask in this regard, as for the appointment of any consultant whose independent view is important, is what sanctions would apply if the consultant fails? Could he be sued? Does he have professional indemnity insurance? Would his business collapse in the event of perceived failure?

Inadequate or Failed Risk Analysis and Management
From these considerations, the following brief 'overview checklist' is presented to help determine whether the risk management process for a project is effective:

- Project Definition. Was the project fully defined before the risk analysis, and have any changes been made since?

- Application of suitable experience. Was the process carried out with the close participation of suitably experienced experts who were able to develop a good understanding of the whole project? Have they confirmed their satisfaction with the report?
- Did the 'expert' involvement in complex and hazardous projects include 'independent' reviewers as defined above?
- Was a codified risk analysis and management process employed?
- Is there a commitment and plan to carry out industry-standard hazard, safety, operability and environmental checks and overview, for the duration of the project and subsequent operation? Have the checks and independent overviews that are possible before project implementation all been adequately and successfully performed and referenced in the Risk report?
- Fatal flaws. Were any risks identified, however unlikely, that cannot be adequately mitigated? These include risks for which mitigation strategies may have been optimised as previously outlined, but the residual Risk, if it occurred, would still be unacceptable.
- Quality assurance. Does the project charter include a commitment to industry-standard QA, under the leadership of a manager who is independent of the project management and Executive?
- Inclusion of mitigating measures. Have the project scope, budget and schedule been updated to include optimised and accepted mitigation measures?

Note that, although application of encoded risk management practice has become the norm for due diligence, there are limitations to the reliability of such practice. Although there are many (and an increasing number) of competent professionals who operate as risk management consultants, for most applications it is very important to have in-depth technical and management experience in the type of project contemplated. A consultant in generic risk management practice may be able to get good results if he receives the full participation of the project team, including any specialist consultants, but this cannot necessarily be taken for granted – especially not if the risk management consultant is foisted onto the team by an Executive who believes he is thereby imposing some sort of discipline. Risk analysis can easily become an unimaginative turn-the-wheel process, resulting in lots of fancy multi-coloured tables and charts with inadequate depth of thought and investigation behind them. Acceptance of the risk management report should be demonstrated by the signature of not only the Project Manager but also the principal project team members (e.g. engineering, procurement, construction, QA, financial and commercial management). It is the project team's report, not just the risk management consultant's report.

There are still all too many major projects in which risks are not identified or are under-estimated, sometimes resulting in tragic consequences. Looking back on such events with 20/20 hindsight, it is all too easy to see that either the risk analysis process was too superficial or that some driving (and usually greedy) entity had been reckless. The common strand of these modes of failure is that the atmosphere for the risk process was wrong. Let's not be too concerned with routine projects such as the construction of water treatment facilities or public buildings. Let's concern ourselves with major projects that involve significant hazards, such as any plant that deals with flammable or hazardous substances, or projects with potentially high social or environmental impact. Let's exercise special care if relatively new technology is employed. The risk process has to be conducted calmly, diligently, dispassionately, with absolutely no pooh-poohing of unwanted suggestions or fear of criticism. All issues raised must be disclosed in the report.

As an example of how the wrong atmosphere can even unintentionally be created, allow me to introduce a brilliant engineer whom we will call Brian Scout. Scout was at the time a Project Manager for Simply Serious Engineering, contractors for major industrial projects. He has a naïve streak, which has persisted even after life's battering. Scout liked to impress his clients and project investors by demonstrating Simply Serious's professionalism. Unless restrained by a more percipient colleague, he would invite the project clients and investors, or their representatives, to come and sit in the risk analysis sessions and verify how well the process was conducted. Result: the project team, the people who best understood the project and its limitations, were apt to clam up completely, rather than expose themselves before these important people. The whole process was undermined.

Similarly, the process is undermined if a major project protagonist in a senior position 'sits in' on the deliberations. A stony-faced CEO driving for project implementation doesn't need to say a word to cause critical issues to be insufficiently considered.

It may be very effective to employ a really critical, experienced and independent reviewer of the process who has a maverick attitude. If it is affordable – and there are some major contractors who would not tender for large fixed-price projects on any other basis – an excellent method of risk analysis is to employ two competitive pre-project teams, who challenge each other.

7. Contingency

Definition, Practices and Abuses

We have ploughed through some issues of estimating and risk management with the main intention of approaching the subject of contingency, one of the pirates' main hunting grounds.

Many widely differing definitions of Contingency exist in fields such as philosophy and law. In this context of project management, its prime usage is to state a cash amount to be added to an estimate to allow for overall cost increases that past experience has shown will be likely to arise out of present uncertainties. (Other usages will be addressed later.)

There have always been, and continue to be, differences in the interpretation of some borderline factors that (according to definition and usage) might be included in the cost-estimating contingency, or alternatively included in the body of the estimate as an 'allowance'. The most common practice is to include in the body of the estimate item costs that are considered to be the most likely (and therefore include any specific item growth expectations), leaving the contingency to deal with any unforeseen increase (or decrease) of the aggregate value. Here's where most of the borderline issues arise: it's often the case that the designer knows from experience (and professional practice) that he has to add an 'allowance' to his estimate of quantities ('bill of materials') to allow for usual growth in that item. For instance, many civil engineers customarily add 7½% to quantities of excavation required, on top of the volume given by simple calculation, to allow for predictable over-excavation. Piping engineers frequently add a similar allowance to compensate for presently incomplete designs. This is a 'growth' allowance that arises out of the methodology of the estimate and should not be included in the contingency. It is an amount required to bring the estimate in line with the most likely value. Well, that's the common practice, but others have different interpretations.

Evidently, to reduce the scope for piracy in this matter, an estimate should be backed up by a fairly detailed and rigorous procedure statement on how the particular estimate was performed. Some guidance on recommended practice is to be found in the various national standards on quantity surveying and the literature of professional bodies such as the Association for Advancement of Cost Engineering International (AACEI).

Another major issue is the list of items that are, in standard practice, excluded from contingency. AACEI, for instance, in the definition of contingency published on their website in 2009, excluded:

1. Major scope changes such as changes in end product specification, capacities, building sizes, and location of the asset or project.
2. Extraordinary events such as major strikes and natural disasters.
3. Management reserves.
4. Escalation and currency effects.

Most other authorities exercise similar practice. I would add to these exceptions: any avoidable significant error or deficiency in the project execution. Is that obvious? It's a very serious matter for organisations that have a history of such failures. People need to be reminded: this estimate assumes near-perfect project execution, and if that's not what is normally achieved, how do we prevent the deviation or allow for it?

An immediate problem arising out of the statement of exclusions is once more the delineation of the borderline. What is a major scope change? What is a significant error? Perhaps this can be dealt with in the estimating procedure statement mentioned above, but it's never easy, and it creates scope for pirates.

Removing these major potential uncertainties from the project estimate increases its accuracy and makes estimating more of a profession and less of a guessing exercise. This, however, is no help to project managers; they still have to achieve an end result, whatever uncertainties may exist. Some very important issues arise out of these exclusions, to be separately discussed in Chapters 10 and 11.

The contingency is usually included as a cash amount at the bottom of the estimate. There are various ways of calculating it – or should I say guessing an appropriate amount? Some methods, particularly the statistically based 'Monte Carlo' simulations, can look very convincing and lend a quantitative basis to the assumption of risk. The output may be expressed as a confidence curve, as per the example below. For a given probability or given confidence limits, a forecast cost can be generated from the curve. For instance, the contingency may be taken as the difference between (a) the cost that there is, say, 90% confidence of not being exceeded, and (b) the cost as per the cost estimate

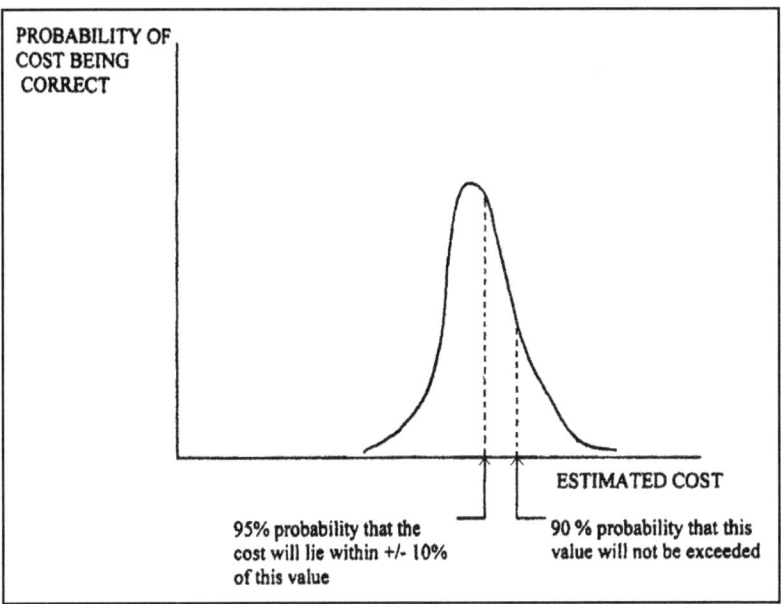

PROBABILITY OF COST BEING CORRECT

ESTIMATED COST

95% probability that the cost will lie within +/- 10% of this value

90 % probability that this value will not be exceeded

Note that 'correct' cost must be defined as lying within a defined bandwidth, say +/–1%, for the probability to have meaning.

There are some drawbacks to this approach, and in fact to all similar statistical approaches. It cannot improve the quality of the information on which the forecast is based. It is possible to build a castle of statistical analysis on a base of guesses and assumptions, and the castle may look deceptively impressive ... until the foundations collapse. The probability calculation can be manipulated. One way is to fail to declare the 'bandwidth' as defined above and use quite a wide bandwidth. Another is to arbitrarily break down the estimate into many components without any more real information to justify the breakdown. Hey presto! The confidence limits (as per statistical analysis) will narrow.

However it is calculated, the amount of cost contingency is based on predicting the future. But the amount required is also heavily dependent on the way in which the estimate was prepared, on the methodology and quality of engineering, and on all the risks that may affect the project and how well they have been identified and mitigated.

We have been dealing with the cost engineer's definition of 'contingency', but the term is applied loosely to embrace a whole universe of often dubious practice. Not just a project manager, but just about everybody, likes having a contingency. It provides more freedom of action and the means to combat unfavourable events. If the contingency comes without sufficiently stringent reporting requirements, it reduces accountability, and that we all like – for ourselves. It is human nature for project performers to make their target easier to meet, not just by access to a declared calculated contingency, but by various 'hidden' contingencies, such as:

a. Using estimate prices that are higher than the minimum. This can be done a number of ways – by not soliciting bids from the most competitive sources at the pre-project stage, by burdening quoted prices with 'allowances' for various deemed deficiencies.
b. Using estimate quantities that are inflated or 'err on the high side'.
c. Failing to optimise engineering design – leaving the opportunity for cost-saving improvements at the project stage.

It is over-simplistic to believe that such practices can easily be eliminated. There is invariably a degree of judgement to be applied when preparing the designs and estimates:

a. As outlined previously, bidders cannot be assumed to provide the most accurate prices for pre-project bids, and often the bid deficiencies are real - the bidders do not quote for exactly what was required and do not accept all the required commercial conditions.

b. When final designs are not yet available, engineers are liable to use quantities which are at the top end of any range of uncertainty. But don't count on it – they may also under-estimate.

c. There is usually no end to the amount that a design can be improved and made to be more cost-effective – if endless time is available (which then makes it uneconomic). This issue is explained in Chapter 9.

The point to be made from these examples is that it is often impossible to prove that an estimate is too costly. An estimate is a forecast of the future; only when the work estimated has been completed and paid for can we know for certain whether the estimate was correct. And even then, there is room for a lot of doubt and controversy. If the estimate is exceeded, maybe the project execution was at fault. If the project came in on budget, maybe the estimate was a self-fulfilling prophecy, about which more later. Surely, an expert reviewer can give an opinion on an estimate, and such a review is usually considered an essential part of finalising an estimate for a large project. There may be mistakes in the estimate, and these can be corrected; but, having corrected the mistakes, we are still left with a judgement, not 'the truth'.

We may arrive at an estimate that is entirely correct according to the estimating procedure adopted, but it can be no better than the procedure.

In a working environment in which stable teams exercise standard and codified methodology, the management may eventually develop a 'feel' for how conservative or adventurous a target has been set. But our present concern is not with conscientious managers; it's with pirates! And they can be sure to exploit every area of uncertainty in one direction. This may be to create easy targets on which to be incentivised, and to incorporate hidden reserves to draw on if they mess up. Or they may 'cut the estimate to the bones', to facilitate the go-ahead for a possibly unjustified project or to win a tender, having worked out a way to grab some up-front reward before making a careful exit in advance of the eventual bad news. (On a long and complex project, such practices can take an amusing if ultimately tragic turn, as another and another over-confident manager takes over, only to experience the need to exit before the publication of progressively worse news becomes unavoidable. This is called 'project pirates liar-dice'!)

The Law of Business Piracy

We have concentrated our attention on cost estimate piracy, having previously looked at project scope piracy. We ought to note in passing another field for the pirate, which is the assumption of excessive technical risk. This may result in an apparently attractive project, whose drawbacks and even possibly complete technical failure will not be noticed until after the project's completion.

In all of these issues, the ultimate question is how to create an organisation in which the pirate has little room to manoeuvre. At the lower levels of an organisation, the need to question contingencies is usually well understood and carried out by codified procedures of supervisory review. The main problem is likely to be at the top of the organisation. Don't believe that any executive, including the CEO, is immune. There is a pirate in all of us; it's just a matter of degree. Just as any politician will become corrupt given unfettered power, so will any executive. Given the pressures of modern business, it's likely that top executives will be more ruthless and piratical than the average employee. That's what it takes to get to the top!

May I propose a 'law of business piracy':

> Any business process tends, over the long run, to be abused by the executive responsible for managing it, to the extent that he is able to evade competition, independent measurement of performance, and accountability.

As a consequence of this 'behaviour at the top', it often happens that the top executive holds for himself a contingency that is not passed on to the next level. This results in sub-optimal performance of the enterprise as a whole. The 'next level' is likely to be driven into unnecessary and damaging false economies through having inadequate contingency. The contingency is an amount that, once decided upon, is a *part of the project budget*, not something that is held back as an exercise of power-play by a pirate Executive. Surely there should be safeguards to ensure that the contingency is spent wisely, like any other item of expenditure. And surely a wise treasury will keep or maintain access to a cash reserve as a super-contingency, not just for the project, but for the organisation as a whole. But don't let that confuse the setting of the project target.

Risk Mitigation, Allowances and Contingency
Note that as defined, the contingency excludes the cost of risk mitigation measures, which have to be included in the project estimate as part of the project delivery. Risk and its mitigation have to be decided upon before contingency is considered. Some project practitioners combine the latter two processes, which is probably harmless as long as each component of mitigation and contingency is properly calculated and the practice is clearly set out and consistent. Confusion may arise (or be created) if a contingency excluding risk mitigation measures is mistaken for one including mitigation. Check this out when reviewing estimates and contingencies.

It is also wise to check that there is a rigid application over the use of individual item estimating 'allowances' purely as an established tool to arrive at the most likely estimate, as previously outlined. Allowances must not include any amount to address the unforeseen or the possibility of failure. Such possibilities should be considered in risk analysis and addressed either by mitigation or addressed in the contingency calculation. With inadequately rigid procedures, a justifiable contingency amount is often doubled up in the body of the estimate and in the stated contingency.

8. Cost Control

Standard Practices and Their Limitations

The importance of this subject in this context is twofold: (a) to note the tie-up with cost-estimating and (b) to overview whether project costs are properly controlled.

At first sight, it seems that, following its acceptance, the project cost estimate becomes the budget and functions simply as the basis for cost control (we'll return to this). As the project progresses, the cost of work is compared with the budget, and if there is any significant increase in a cost component, management action may be taken to rectify the deviation; and in any event a revised cost forecast may be issued for review and action by higher management.

To perform any useful function, the cost controller or cost engineer clearly has to have a budget that is suitably broken down, a system for receiving and recording cost data as the project evolves, and some number-crunching process or software that makes comparisons with itemised budget costs and ultimately produces management reports. But that is just a framework. The reality is that he can do all of this and be completely ineffective. Costs can only be *controlled* when making the decisions by which costs are incurred, including, for each project component, decisions about specification, design, procurement and construction. The people actually performing these unit operations are the people who can control costs. They are mainly engineers and technicians.

The potential effectiveness of cost control is limited by, and may be verified by:

1. The degree to which the project is broken down into work packages that satisfy the following criteria:
   - The packages are small enough that they will be completed quite soon after their commencement. In this context, 'time to completion' means the time from commencing a task to arriving at a cost commitment, e.g. from starting an engineering design until having a completed design with a bill of quantities, which can be compared with the budget case.
   - Each package carries a realistic budget cost (which could also be expressed in tons of steelwork or man-hours, etc.).
   - The packages accurately represent the way in which work is actually done. It is no good for instance having a pipework budget broken down only into totalled quantities of pipes and fittings of each type and size, or a steelwork estimate broken down only into the total tonnage of each type of steel plate or section. The items may be purchased in bulk that way, and their costs can be rolled up into estimates that way, but the items are not designed or built that way. They're designed and built by individual pipeline or functional structure, and have to be budgeted like that for cost to be controllable.
2. The time from when decisions affecting cost are provisionally taken, until when cost feedback is available. The designer or constructor should know exactly the budget case (not just the budget cost, but the anticipated design and methodology for the budget case) before commencing a task or making a commitment. The comparison with budget must be made before the task is considered to be complete and before going on to the next stage of commitment. It's no good waiting until the procurement offers arrive, or worse until the invoices arrive; it's usually too late to make a change.

Self-Fulfilling Prophecies
Reverting to the remarks about estimate usage at the beginning of this chapter, it should be evident that in the long run there is a chicken-and-egg relationship with the final reported cost. The cost is controlled against the estimate, but the estimate anticipates the final cost, which is used as the main basis for the next project estimate. Without suitable intervention, it is possible within an organisation that the estimate becomes a self-fulfilling prophecy, because there is always enough meat in it that completion within budget is possible. We've considered above some of the many, many circumstances that can cause final cost to deviate from estimated cost. If an organisation has a record of projects coming in close to budget, that may be an indication of management efficiency. But it's just as likely to be an indicator of excessive contingencies or flexible scope definition. If that is the case, what is happening to the cash that should be saved on the projects that have few mishaps, and why are no projects coming in well below budget? Where has the treasure chest of savings been hidden? Or has it already been dissipated in the form of various performance bonuses and perks?

Even worse, have potential savings been lost to the project's suppliers and contractors, following an insufficiently competitive procurement process carried out in the knowledge that the project budget would not be exceeded? Possibly lost to suppliers participating in a 'partnering' process – happy, prosperous suppliers, with whom the Owner's executives enjoy 'a good, steady relationship'?

Wider Aspects of Management Inadequacy
The previous observations serve to underline the observation that cost control and cost reporting are subsets of wider issues of project management; inadequate project management results in inadequate cost control and possibly runaway costs. There is nothing much that cost controllers can do about this other than chart the progress of failure, and they may have difficulty in doing even that if the cost budgets have not been set up properly, as noted above.

There has long been a class of projects in which the project definition or degree of completeness of the pre-project study has been too superficial. Maybe only in certain respects: some of the 'usual suspects' here include failure to properly perform all elements of technical, infrastructural, environmental and market studies; skimped pre-project engineering and management planning; over-optimistic estimating and risk analysis. Such failure may arise from incompetence, or there may be some direction to these happenings, some executive influence. In the latter case, there is a built-in likelihood that project failure will not be detected or reported until an advanced stage of the project, because in effect the project performance will be tracked against a model that itself incorporates in-built failures. Before further discussion of this important theme, it is beneficial to consider that other major project constraint, time.

9. … and Project Planning and Scheduling Are Also Subject to Abuse

The Determination of Project Schedule, and Its Abuse

Reader, please excuse me for beginning this section with a little philosophising on a subject that fascinates me.

The issues of scope, quality, cost and time are intertwined and interreact in the performance of a project. They are the principle parameters of project definition, and can be regarded as the highest level constraints on performance. To quote an old project management maxim, take away any one of these constraints and the project execution becomes dead easy. At board level the constraint of time (or project schedule) is possibly the least understood, because it is (for all of us) the hardest to grasp. Surely directors are well aware of the often costly and damaging effects of failure to perform according to required schedule. Performance according to plan is a must for any multi-functional entity, and failure to do so is simply chaos. However, setting the project schedule at its outset is another matter, and usually carries major implications. Optimal performance of schedule setting, like the comparison of project alternatives discussed in Chapter 2, can only be effectively overseen at the pre-project stage.

There is a similarity between the application of engineering and management effort to a project (which will here be shortened to 'engineering') and the allocation of time for its completion. Considering first engineering, there is a practical minimum amount without which project execution is impossible. More effort than the minimum (if effectively used) should reduce the project's total cost (i.e. the direct field cost plus the engineering cost) by designing things more economically, smarter procurement, and better organised construction. But there comes a point at which additional engineering effort costs more than the benefit. The curve of total cost versus engineering effort has a minimum, which may be considered to be the economic optimum *if other factors such as time are not included in the equation.*

In the same way, there is a practical minimum time in which the project may be executed, but a project executed in too much of a hurry is very expensive. There's no time for arriving at the best designs, no time to shop around; lots more people are needed for construction (with the added costs of establishing them on site), and they get in each other's way. As more time is made available, the overall costs should be reduced, but there comes a point at which needless expense is incurred and overall costs begin to increase. Purely to illustrate the point:

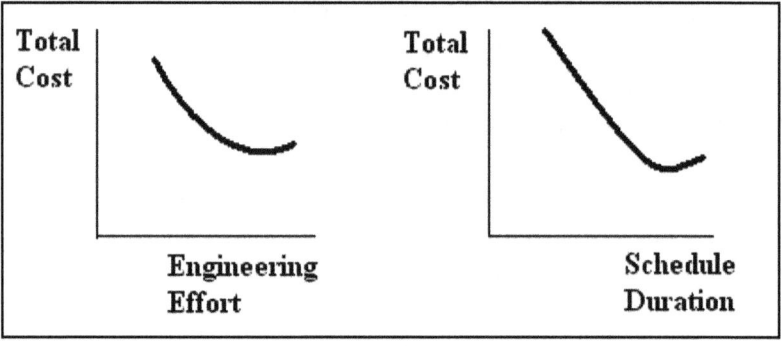

The real situation is more complex, as these and other factors inevitably interact. The operational costs and revenues after project completion must be considered as well as the project cost, and these costs and revenues are also related to the time to complete the project. The engineering effort and the duration of the project schedule are also related to each other. In fact the whole economic model, including project and post-project operation, must be taken into consideration to optimise the project performance.

For the Project Manager, time is money, but lack of time likely costs even more money. It can be very expensive to have to negotiate deals and make commitments under too much pressure of time. So the Project Manager needs a time contingency as well as a cash contingency to operate effectively, and the calculation (or should I say judgement?) of the time contingency is just as important as the calculation of cost contingency. And subject to the same levels of abuse.

The Importance of Board Performance

For many large organisations, enterprises and government departments alike, the process of approval of large projects is manifestly the greatest waste of the asset of time. Consider a large project for which the pre-feasibility and feasibility studies take two years. A Board presentation is made, but it is decided that various changes are required. After all, what is a Board for, if only to rubber-stamp management plans? A further year elapses (in intervals of three months – the Board only sits three-monthly) before the project is approved. (In the intervening period the project circumstances have changed, the planning is not quite up to date and contractors' commitments are less firm, making it more difficult to execute the project as per plan and budget.) If only three months of this year's delay, or even a month, were available to extend the schedule, that could lead to a significant improvement of project performance. But what does the Board do – it probably demands a schedule reduction to make up for lost time! ('The bastards wasted twelve months, and now they want it yesterday', the project team will be heard to say!)

The preceding scenario illustrates the advantage held by the owner-manager of an enterprise – provided he really is managing. Clearly the functioning and decision-making process of the Board, and if necessary its interaction with shareholders, is an integral part of the competitiveness of the enterprise as a whole and needs to be analysed and improved to the necessary levels of performance. This can only come about if the directors interact throughout the pre-project period, such that the eventual approval process is a timed project event, just like any other project milestone. It is hardly likely to come about if decision-making directors are remote entities who gather in club-like fashion once every three months to have their egos massaged.

Overall Project Management Failure

Reverting to where we left off in the previous chapter, the constraints of cost and time – and their abuse – usually have to be considered together. A project that runs out of time usually runs out of money also. Sometimes this happens because the underlying management problems, such as failure to recognise inherent shortcomings, affect both, and sometimes because management action to correct perceived shortcomings takes the form of compromise between cost and time issues.

A semi-serious view of major failed projects is that the first 80% of the project scope is achieved within 80% of the cost budget and 80% of the allotted time schedule. Then the final 80% of the project scope (much of which may be a rework of the original scope) is achieved at the expense of another 80% of the project cost budget and another 80% of the allotted schedule duration.

Frequently, the activities and corresponding cost and time expenditure incurred in the 'final 80%' stage are somewhat disorganised, are performed rather ineffectually, could have been performed at half the additional time and cost. But what often happens is that, following the late understanding that a project has failed, the Owner or the top management of a project contractor takes one reactive step after another, without properly addressing the underlying issues. These reactive steps are likely to include replacement of the project management.

A Project Manager or other performer, who knows or suspects that he may be replaced, is unlikely to make full disclosure of under-performance, especially when it can be dressed up and sold on to a replacement in 'liar-dice' fashion. The replacement is likely to be picked on the basis of willingness to, even of boasting his ability to 'sort out this mess'. His scope for simply unconstructively trashing all work done to date is rather limited; the Owner will require a commitment to turn matters around before appointing him.

Consider now how this scenario looks to a Project Manager who is aware that he is likely to be fired and replaced. If his replacement fails to bring the project back on track, there may be a perception that it was more problematic than was originally acknowledged. The original manager may even subsequently argue that the project failed because of his untimely replacement! On the other hand, subsequent success of the project may be taken to confirm the original manager's inadequacy.

In such circumstances, can an outgoing manager really be expected to fully disclose all problems that, by now, he should understand better than anybody?

In conclusion:

- Project failure, and especially major failure, is often caused by inadequate pre-project work. This may result in misdirection of the subsequent work, and also in failure of the project controls, resulting in rather late reporting of unacceptable performance.
- If there are any indications of non-performance, it is important to address not only the actual non-performance but any possible underlying deficiencies, and especially those relating to the pre-project work and the setting of the 'project baseline'. It is never too late to revisit and re-evaluate the project fundamentals and especially the setting of those against which project performance is measured.
- At any point in the project, but especially when contemplating or actually instituting the handover of project responsibilities from one party to another, it is desirable to perform an independent assessment of the project, including its fundamentals. This assessment should *not* be entrusted solely to a party targeted to take over the project roles being assessed.

The Cost–Revenue Spreadsheet

In Chapter 4 we noted that the second major spreadsheet used to define the performance of a project is the cost–revenue (or cash flow) spreadsheet. This should not just be regarded as an accountant's tool. It is also a very useful tool for checking whether a project is being performed on track, by comparing the current cost–revenue spreadsheet with the project definition case.

There are a number of reasons this comparison is useful:

1. It provides a final, effective and hard-to- manipulate indicator of project performance. Deviations from the overall project plan and schedule, whatever the cause, all tend to have consequences that are reflected in this spreadsheet comparison in stark and unalterable contrast. If an activity has not been paid for, it

probably hasn't been completed. If it has been performed incorrectly, the Project Manager is unlikely to have paid for it.

2. The cost report versus budget spreadsheet comparison is not nearly so useful for this purpose, because the figures include forecasts and allowances that reflect 'views' that are opinionative and can be manipulated. The current cost–revenue spreadsheet is put together from cash flow data gathered quite independently of physical progress reports. It is purely a financial accounting document, and any manipulation is likely to be regarded as criminal fraud, with consequent risk of prosecution – an outcome which is outside the scope of this book. Our focus is on fringe delinquency that is not regarded as criminal practice.

3. Aside from fraudulent accounting, an unscrupulous project manager could cook the books by making unwarranted advance payments to contractors and suppliers, or by delaying payment without justification. The project procedures should sufficiently define the protocols of payment, usually by a system of certification, so that any such attempts will be seen as potentially criminal practice by the project team members, and be resisted or reported.

Clearly, the performance of this useful project performance check is critically dependent on the care with which the initial cash flow forecast was performed, and particularly the precise and detailed correspondence of the cash flow budget to the cost budget spreadsheet. Too often this is not the case; major projects are authorised without much concern about the cash flow spreadsheet, which is a rough-and-ready assemblage put together simply to ensure that enough cash will be available when required. In the extreme case, there is no real project cash flow plan at all; the project Executive is simply voted an adequate amount of money at the outset – and a pirate is left with many avenues to enhance reported performance, including:

- gaining unbudgeted interest on unused funds;
- agreeing generous advance payment terms for contracts in return for an overall price discount, thereby reducing non-time-related reported final costs;

- eliminating an important tool for independently tracking project performance.

Inferences to be drawn from comparing cash flow with budget have limitations. However carefully the budget case may have been put together, it is never perfect and is apt to include time contingencies as well as cash contingencies, with all the associated potential for abuse. The need to demonstrate schedule compliance by performing as per the cost-revenue spreadsheet should not be allowed to encourage the Project Manager to forego opportunities to improve cash flow, such as justifiably holding back payments to suppliers.

In conclusion, this project-tracking device should be seen as an alarm, not a verdict, which should be based on detailed study of the deviation that sets off the alarm.

The Treasure Chest

Ideally, the cost contingency should be time -based and reflected as such in the cost–revenue spreadsheet, so that deviation over time can be noted of what was allowed from what was spent. Any movement should have an explanation. Note that the contingency included in the cost forecast should decrease as the project advances and uncertainties are reduced or become historical certainties.

The previous chapter drew attention to the possible abuse of a 'hidden treasure-chest' of savings arising from a project budget based on an over-generous estimate or excessive contingency. It is always necessary to be on the lookout for such practice. One of the best methods is by regular review of contingency, including its periodic recalculation following detailed update of the specific uncertainties on which it was based. Any excess contingency that arises from the update should be promptly reallocated to a project profit forecast or a visible corporate savings account. These are corporate savings, not the Project Manager's savings to be spent to personal advantage. And at corporate level they are not to be used to cover up deficiencies in other projects or operations, or to be spent on a host of unauthorised and unauthorisable possibilities.

It is not uncommon for an organisation that is heavily involved in projects to manipulate unspent project contingencies to 'smooth out' corporate financial performance over successive periods of reporting.

Contingency 'calculation' is always a matter of opinion rather than fact, and therefore open to manipulation. In extreme cases, the 'contingency' in project reports may be found to be an amount determined by corporate intervention with little reference to project realities. This may be considered to be a valid way of running the business in the shareholders' interests (if not those of the national exchequer) by reducing tax liabilities, or by reducing share-price volatility, but the practice may also be contrary to shareholders' interests, or contrary to the interests of certain minority shareholders, an issue to which we will return.

10. Force Majeure

Explanation, Definition and Pitfalls

In the definition of contingency given in Chapter 7, we noted that it is usual practice to exclude from the contingency 'extraordinary events such as major strikes and natural disaster ... escalation and currency effects'. Noting that provision of contingency is one of the prime tools to manage such unexpected events, how can this be?

Extraordinary events do happen from time to time (I shall refer to them as 'force majeure'). Escalation (inflation) is practically inevitable, although prices (for the same commodity) do decrease sometimes. Currency effects (forex variation) are also inevitable in the modern global economy. Excluding these effects from the contingency implies that they are also excluded from the budget, which is easily extended to mean excluded from the Project Manager's accountability. How can this be, when the effects can be major, even decisive, to the project's outcome?

Some major organisations do in fact consider it to be unreasonable to hold the Project Manager accountable for events outside his control, and so they remove consideration of these effects from project targets and, as applicable, have them reported separately. Well, that's the reasoning you will usually be given to justify such practice, but in my opinion the management attitude portrayed by such reasoning is pathetic and insupportable. A project's performance is affected by very many factors, and it's the Project Manager's responsibility to manage them all. And he usually needs to optimise, to trade off one effect against another to get the best overall result. Which he's likely to neglect in a situation where he might have to sacrifice some performance on the items for which he's held accountable, in favour of dealing with problems for which he's not held accountable.

This chapter will outline some issues relating to force majeure, mainly practical issues of project engineering and construction. The next chapter addresses similar issues of inflation and forex variation, which reside more in the domain of project accounting. What all these issues have in common is that it may be claimed that fundamental underlying uncertainties entail that there should be some relaxation of accountability on the part of the project performer. Start with this precept and one can rapidly embark on a slippery slope where there is little accountability at all for such events, and where consequently a whole fleet of pirates (or flock of vultures) may grab the opportunities thereby created.

A force majeure event will inevitably throw out a huge challenge to the Project Manager and be very costly to the Owner. How well the Project Manager performs in mitigating the risk and managing the event is an extremely important measure of his performance. How can he not be held accountable for this? Absurd.

Project Management of Force Majeure

Force majeure is fundamentally a legal concept, in which it is considered to be unreasonable to hold a contracting party responsible for an event that can be neither anticipated nor controlled. Since there are two parties to a contract (sometimes more), it is usually held that both parties lose their right to claim against each other on grounds of any consequences of the event. More simply, each party will pick up its own costs arising out of the event, but there will be no penalties for non-performance caused by the event, and in particular no penalties for consequent delays. This is usual, but actual legal interpretation depends on the legal jurisdiction and of course on any agreed specific contractual provisions, to the extent that such agreed provisions may be legally binding. Some standard contract conditions such as Fidic[6] also require

---

6   The international association of consulting engineers, which issues several
model conditions of contract.

that defined costs incurred by the contractor may be payable by the Owner under certain circumstances. So what are the Executive's and Project Manager's responsibilities?

Risk Analysis and Management of Force Majeure
The responsibilities start with pre-project risk evaluation. No reasonably possible threat can be excluded just because it is classifiable as force majeure. Note that the events must be considered to be unlikely, within the lifetime of the project works, to be classified as force majeure at all (we will return to this). We shall skip the processes of risk identification and impact evaluation, and assume that after a competent risk analysis process we are dealing with identified Risks, however unlikely, that may be unacceptably damaging in their impact. We have tacitly excluded risks that cannot be identified *by any diligent process*, the 'unknown unknown' risks (as they are usually classified, with my apologies). I will accept that there's not much to be done about these (except resort to prayer) until there is an indication that they may happen, unless an insurer is to be found for such nebulous concerns.

Possible force majeure events can be classified into the following groups by likelihood. They range from

a. Events that are known to have happened in the past, not neces-sarily near the same location, and could happen again, but for which there is no accepted way to determine the possible likeli-hood or timing. Examples: riotous civil unrest following random political assassination in a politically stable country; meteor impact.

to

b. Events for which it is possible for an appropriate expert to quan-tify the likelihood of the event happening within a given period of time. Examples are the use of statistics from which it is pos-sible to define and quantify such possibilities as a 50-year wave or a 100-year wind.

In between:

c. There are many types of event that may or may not be inherently uncertain, such as war, earthquake, strikes. In some countries and circumstances, the risk is greater than in others. The 'inherent' uncertainty in these cases may be qualified to remark that it is difficult to quantify the uncertainty, but it is manifest that in some places, at some times, under some circumstances, the risk is greater than at others.

For practical purposes, it is reasonable to exclude class (a) events from mitigation commitment, but it should be noted that there is usually some warning, closer to the time, of such an impending event. If there is such warning, it is clearly the responsibility of the Project Manager to take note and revise the risk analysis and possible mitigation plans without delay. Further, it is his responsibility to be on the lookout for, and receptive to, the warning signs, whether they be a change in the political environment, unusual weather phenomena, or earth tremors. As remarked previously, if he's not held responsible for force majeure events, he may be tempted to refrain from taking funds and resources from his contingency to mitigate the risk as it develops.

Type (b) events can be analysed on the basis of quantified risk evaluation (Risk = probability × impact) and the comparison of any possible mitigation cost (usually change of design or construction plan, or insurance) with the Risk. This may be performed on a discounted cash flow basis, where appropriate. The best scenario may be chosen; in general, the optimum case is when the marginal decrease in Risk becomes less than the marginal cost increase of mitigating measures, as outlined in Chapter 6. By such means may be determined, for instance, the amount it is worth spending on structural reinforcement to combat very high winds, and arriving at the corresponding wind value above which failure may occur.

To put it more simply, the Project Manager should not be encouraged to economise on relatively inexpensive measures that may reduce or eliminate a major force majeure Risk. But you won't approach this optimum design if any wind above the standard design case is simply regarded as a force majeure event, an 'act of God' with consequences which no mortal is responsible for managing!

Type (c) events should be analysed in the same fashion wherever possible, even though in a necessarily rough and ready way. At least the obvious alternatives should be considered and acted upon. For instance, whyever carry out a project in a historically uncertain place or during an unpropitious time or circumstance, when less risky alternatives are available at little additional cost?

Contractual Definition

The wording relating to force majeure, to be used in all of the project's contracts, is of extreme importance, in any legal jurisdiction. The wording must reflect the exact sharing of risk to be agreed between the contracting parties. The essence of this agreement is the definition of what constitutes a force majeure event, and in that case what are the obligations and rights of each party. We are looking at this as an Owner, and would wish for the contractor to accept as much responsibility as can be negotiated *and enforced*.

It is extremely important to make the definition absolutely clear, in quantitative terms where possible, and including the obligation of diligence on any contractor to conduct adequate research and take all appropriate measures to mitigate risk. Such clarity must include careful legal review and wording to suit countries which may have legal jurisdiction. Many of the issues that require clarity are ones that can be addressed by quantification. For instance, if a possible threshold wind condition is going to be contractually accepted to define a force majeure event, quantify the strength of that wind, the standard by which the wind strength will be defined and measured, the means of measurement that will be employed, the party responsible for the measurement, and the fallback if that party fails in its responsibility. Having defined the limiting force majeure condition, the next requirement is to define exactly the responsibilities and liabilities of each party in the event that the condition does in fact materialise and cause damage.

Force Majeure Plastique

The importance of definition has been emphasised because 'events beyond my control' are so frequently the excuse for failure, a justification that conceals insufficient anticipation, mitigation and planning for unwanted events, and also of the responsibility for managing the consequences.

Sometimes, indeed, the events are not unwanted at all; they may be a heaven-sent opportunity for a project participant to be relieved of responsibility for embarking on an inherently flawed project, for accepting an unachievable target, or simply for the consequences of poor performance.

In the event of a dispute about responsibilities following a force majeure event, or more usually an event that by some stretch of chari-table imagination might be classed as force majeure, the litigant seek-ing relief usually bases his argument on the need for 'fairness'. Having established that he was not totally remiss in anticipating the event, why should he be penalised, irrespective of what it says in the contract? In several legal jurisdictions, contract provisions considered to be unfair may be set aside by a court. Indeed, this may not be a matter for a court or arbitrator; on occasion the Owner's representatives (usually construc-tion management who have not participated in the contract negotiation) may simply make concessions unwarranted by a contract, on the basis of perceived fairness. In this case, often the construction management (a profession noted for behaviour values along established norms) may regard deviation from standard contractual responsibilities as unfair, with no regard for what may have been negotiated under competitive circumstances. In both legal and management practice, what has been agreed may be replaced by what is considered to be fair.

Given the real possibility that obligations relating to a force majeure event, or something that may be claimed to be one, may be negated or diluted by judges of 'fairness', the project Owner should be well advised not to rely on such contractual provisions alone. Perhaps he should instead directly cause prudent mitigation to be exercised, within the scope of the contractor's work. Investigate, describe and quantify whatever relevant factors may be a cause for concern *to the contrac-tor also*. Decide on the mitigating actions required, decide on the con-tingency plans required and incorporate the required performance of these actions and plans into the contract scope. Take or enforce direct action, rather than rely on a contractor who may be quite happy to gam-ble on the non-occurrence of events which might be classified as force majeure – an outcome that a sympathetic judge might regard as beyond the bounds of the contractor's responsibility.

And once again, none of this will happen in an environment in which force majeure is regarded as a valid cop-out for the Executive and the Project Manager.

11. The Other Two Frequent Cop-outs: Inflation and Forex Variation

Inflation

It is very difficult to measure the effect of inflation on project performance, yet some organisations go to great lengths to attempt this, such as stating the project budget in '2001 $US'. Now I happen to have a 2001 series $10 banknote. It is now worth – exactly $10! There's no such thing as a 2001 dollar; there's only a dollar. Surely, as we considered in Chapter 4, the buying power of money will change and will usually decrease. That is usually in some measure compensated by the interest earned by unexpended cash, which in turn relates to the discount rate used in the economic analysis spreadsheet.

Inflation cannot be ignored or its consequences excused, or its effects are likely to be sub-optimally managed. Any attempt to remove inflationary effects from the project performance equation should be viewed with extreme care. Aside from any other considerations, it is usually impossible to determine how much of an item price increase is caused by inflation. Some commodity and labour prices are linked to published industry indices, and some contractors may be prepared to enter into long-term contracts on the basis of price adjustment according to published indices. Indices are often invaluable for this purpose, but they cannot diminish the responsibility of the Project Manager to make the best of any inflationary circumstances. Rather, base the target project cost and cash flow spreadsheets on stated cost inflation (and interest and discount rate) assumptions, and hold the Project Manager responsible for achieving or bettering these targets under whatever inflationary circumstances arise – because this is what the enterprise really needs.

Forex Variations

At first glance forex variation may seem rather similar to inflation in its effect on the project, but there are some important differences. In particular, exchange rate variations tend to move much more quickly than inflation, are less predictable and, for the more stable currencies at least, are likely to move in both directions. By way of mitigation, it is usually possible to hedge, by effectively buying the required currency forward, but project management issues may arise if the hedging is carried out too remotely from the project, e.g. by a central treasury function. Depending on the way that the treasury–project relationship has been set up, the Project Manager can find himself virtually compelled to purchase from a certain country, when a switch might yield better value. The Project Manager's ability to get better project deals may be unnecessarily restricted, or he may find that following the corporate line (and making his own project report look better) actually disadvantages the enterprise. The following example is an attempt to illustrate this.

It is quite usual at the outset of the project to have a budget broken down into various currencies, but there is usually little advance commitment as to who the suppliers and contractors will be. Naturally; the more freedom of sourcing, the better the competition to get the best deals. Consider a project to build a major enterprise for a global entity in a developing country with a weak currency. The enterprise, as per usual practice, conducted its corporate and project accounting in a major foreign currency, US$. At the time of preparing the budget estimate, a major item of machinery – say, a big generator – was intended to be sourced from the USA and was included under US$ expenditure. After project authorisation, and by the time that the project engineers had finalised their purchasing documentation and were ready to place an order, several months had elapsed and the dollar had significantly strengthened against the yen. At current exchange rates it would have been much cheaper (still in dollar terms) to buy the item in Japan. But according to the fixed-exchange-rate project accounting system, the Japanese supplier was evaluated at the old exchange rate and still looked more expensive. The project report would show a higher cost if this economical purchase switch was made!

A simple high-cost absurdity like this may possibly be corrected by management agreement, but how many more minor items might be suboptimally purchased?

There are some other issues of manageability. Some purchased items are made up of components that are multi-national in origin, making it quite difficult to separate out the currency components. Corresponding to multiple exchange rate variations, there will just be a price change that cannot readily be differentiated from inflation. The prices of pre-imported stock items will not necessarily immediately follow exchange rate variations, and, just to complicate matters, prices may follow the 'sticky-downward' path as exchange rates become more favourable.

Considering all of the above, it is my opinion that attempts to remove forex variation effects from project reports (and, correspondingly, the Project Manager's responsibility) are often a mistake. There may be exceptions where the nature of the project and its external circumstances indicate otherwise. It may often be wise to hedge by buying appropriate currencies forward, but it should be a reasoned decision based on a high level of confidence that those currencies will actually be required. And of course few people would be foolish enough to leave funds in a weak currency when alternatives are available. The Project Manager must be discouraged from doing this – but is not if such losses are simply 'taken out of the equation.' Another absurdity.

Conclusion

For the management of all three of these issues, to remove the effects of particular cost variations from project reporting creates a situation which does not address reality. Costs vary, and no-one is accountable for taking mitigating action, or taking advantage of benefits that may become available. The consequent accountability cop-outs create space for pirates to move. Executives are apt to exercise the discretion available by taking responsibility away from the project in dubious ways, e.g. by creating a twilight accounting department where all currency exchange decisions and transactions are made, without full appreciation of the project implications. Sooner or later, this department turns into an outright gambling den, where fortunes (and individual bonuses) are made and enterprises are sunk.

The Project Manager should be held responsible for managing these items, and their effects should not be excluded from project financial reporting. If it is consequently found necessary to bolster the project team with some very specialist advisers, well and good. Far better to provide this specialist service within the project team, or from consultants managed by the project team, rather than from an independent source.

12. Ethics and Corruption: A Fourth Major Uncertainty

Why This Subject Is Particularly Contentious
The next few chapters will examine aspects of project procurement, sub-contracting and outsourcing, in which a frequent underlying issue is the concept of ethical behaviour and its antithesis, corruption. It makes sense to discuss this subject first.

Many businessmen and politicians are uncomfortable about publicly discussing such issues, and with good reason, which we will address. It is easy to dismiss 'corruption' as simple criminality: non-conformance to a set of rules designed to regulate business practice in accordance with ethical principles. Especially in a global context, the subject is infinitely more complex, fundamentally because different societies have different ethical principles (if any) and different laws with different interpretations. Even in a single nation, there are always differences in ethical values and expectations, especially between the 'haves' and the 'have-nots'. In the world as a whole, the complexity of the situation presents major challenges to the execution of international projects. Behind these challenges lie uncertainties arising from the lack of any standard business practices relating to activities that are not disclosed publicly; which cannot be disclosed publicly. It is easy for project Executives to shy away from these challenges, as from other uncertainties such as inflation, currency variation and force majeure. Once again, glossing over such a major issue simply creates opportunities for pirates. We cannot ignore this subject in the present context.

This primer attempts to outline some basic 'corrupt' practices, review how the issues are often handled, and draw some conclusions on how best to deal with them. The starting point is to acknowledge that there is no such thing as a universal moral or legal code, but that there are plenty of nations, religions and individuals who believe either that their code is the only legitimate code, or possibly that there is no legitimate code. There are plenty of societies that regard outsiders as fair game for unfair, dishonest or criminal practice. (Not just in under-developed countries: for example, a basic premise of US anti-trust legislation was that dealings with foreign countries were exempted. US anti-terrorist policies, in so far as they have been disclosed, have sanctioned the extra-judicial killing of foreigners, but not US citizens.)

There are plenty of lawyers and politicians who see opportunities to elevate themselves as international arbiters of what is right and what is wrong, sometimes with disastrous consequences. And plenty of hypocrites, at all levels, who say one thing and practise another. This is the actual environment within which the international project Executive has to operate and compete.

A Widespread Practice

In a global business environment fundamentally driven by greed, corruption is inevitable. The degree of corruption should not be gauged by criminal statistics – apart from the fact that prosecutions for this offence are very low compared with the actual activity, statistical study is practically impossible because of a widely varied understanding of what constitutes corruption.

'Corruption' is a term that is very broadly applied, and difficult to define. Some morally very upright people are inclined to apply the term to what others would regard as justifiable business practice, such as taking full advantage of non-competitive opportunities when these may arise or legally be created. In the following the term will be restricted to the soliciting, offering and acceptance of cash or kind in return for the improper exercise of authority. 'Improper' leads to further problems of definition; it seems we have to fall back on whatever is defined as criminal practice according to the laws of the countries involved, or to behaviour which contravenes the defined ethical code for an executive or official. But that again raises questions of interpretation, when legal systems and both private and public administrations differ and may themselves be corrupt.

The preceding paragraph is not of much assistance when searching for a definition of corruption, but that is intentional; the point being made is that there is no globally accepted definition or even understanding, and that is crucial to this chapter.

To the people of many 'first world' countries, 'corruption' is, with certain exceptions, what happens in other countries, in particular African, Latin American and Asian countries. The exceptions that they acknowledge include overtly criminal behaviour within their own country, which they expect to be combated by the police with ensuing prosecution and penalty. They are wrong to believe that these are the only exceptions within their own countries. There are many more instances, which are often more subtle and borderline in classification. Borderline issues represent a real challenge to the business executive: stray too far on one side of a border and face indictment for criminality and the trashing of a company's name; stray too far on the other side and become uncompetitive in many situations. And not just uncompetitive; maybe end up in a third-world prison on trumped-up charges, after failing to pay what local powers believe to be their just dues. Or, more often, see that fate suffered by employees who are in effect held to ransom by officials of the host government. Executives who spend too much effort (publicly) in trying to delineate the border may already be regarded as indulging in sharp practice and suffer damage to their reputation or loss of opportunities. Fundamentally, this comes about because there is usually a range of opinion on where that border should be.

In many (maybe all) African countries, on which I shall concentrate on the basis of personal experience, corruption is practically a perk of office. In some countries, it exists at a lower level as a substitute for paying civil servants, including policemen, a living wage. At the higher levels of office, it becomes the means of creation of extreme wealth, usually in offshore accounts, for the rulers.

At the lower end of corrupt practice, it can be impossible for an individual to travel from A to B without paying some form of bribe to an official, or to an extortionist shielded by officials. Or to complete any type of official transaction, including obtaining any one of a myriad of permits and licences needed to exist and earn income. Or even to paint the exterior of a building.

Although in some cases the bribe solicitors may be very confident and brazen, demanding exactly what they want, Africans tend to be more devious.

'You want the permit you applied for? No, it's not here. I am still waiting for form X and signature from Y.'

'So how come others got their permit ahead of me?'

A shrug, or a further vague explanation. 'Come back tomorrow'.

The process will be repeated indefinitely, until the bribe, and the right bribe, is *offered*. It is not solicited; it is up to the briber to make the first overt approach, to put himself in the wrong. Of course, there is usually no lack of local 'advisers' or 'agents' willing to guide him through the process or 'front' for him, in exchange for a 'commission'. But in the first place, he probably discovers this need the hard way.

The same methodology often applies to big contracts, private and government. Even if it's a private enterprise deal, government parties will be involved somehow in the authorisation. Anybody who has the power to make a decision (or his superior) will need to be paid off somehow, and the higher the value of the deal, the higher the level of the officials and politicians involved. That's the system, and it's up to the briber to come up with an offer in cash or kind, with probably some hints from advisers to help matters along. Or to work through a commission-taking agency acting as intermediary. But seldom a 'pay me this and I'll do that' from the principals behind the deal. It's up to the foreign party to find out how business may be successfully conducted, usually through an initial approach by an intermediary.

Some Standard Methodology

It is quite fashionable for Western companies to try to avoid bribery payment to individuals and instead contribute to the coffers of the ruling party. This is of course an indirect way of doing the same thing, and they know it. The ruling party is invariably corrupt, and most of the money will quickly find its way to its leaders. At this level, the shades of difference between this and political donations in Western countries cannot easily be demarcated. This methodology is limited to high-level applications, which the political leadership is both interested in and able to control. There are very many lower-level matters that require a different approach.

Another method is simply to appoint an independent 'local agent' whose job is to 'take care' of certain transactions without (at least, officially) defining how he goes about it. The transactions could include facilitating the passage of individuals from A to B, getting malicious government officials to go away, or securing business. The give-away as to what the agent is actually doing is that the amount he is paid may seem exorbitant for the services rendered. The trail can usually be confused by combining the agent's operations with those of local sub-contractors. Another method is to employ and pay the agent through an entirely separate offshore organisation owned by the same shareholders.

Sometimes rather little is done to hide 'commissions', but people still get away with it. Consider the case of that very sound but naïve engineer and contractor's Project Manager, Brian Scout. Scout would receive from his Marketing Department the budget for a major project in the countries of the former Soviet Union, and get to the line above the bottom: 'Z office commission, 12%.'

'This is ridiculous,' he would say. 'How can Z possibly be worth that much? What are they going to do for that money? $12 million on a $100 million project?'

Scout knew very well that Z could actually do very little to help the project execution. According to local taxation practice, any overt project execution participation would change the status of Z from 'representative office' to 'project office' and incur a severe withholding tax penalty. But Scout would go on and on trying to get Z to take up tasks to 'earn their money', thereby causing considerable discomfort to a few key executives who didn't appreciate the publicising of this statistic. But nobody was going to enlighten Scout on the underlying secret: there was a firm policy among those within the small complicit circle that such matters should not be mentioned or discussed. Poor old Scout, able and diligent fellow that he was, he never did reach his full potential.

Besides commissions, there are countless methods of transferring wealth in a way that can be classified as legitimate, such as buying project components at inflated prices from shadowy entities that are just a front for the real producers. Surprise, surprise, these shadowy entities are inevitably able somehow to provide influence in favour of the pur-chasers. The South African government has recently developed this practice to an art form, under the banner of 'Black Empowerment', a title designed to give the process some sort of moral legitimacy by asso-ciation with affirmative action. But in most other African countries, no such art form is necessary, because law enforcement and the legal sys-tem are themselves corrupt and subservient to the ruling party.[7] (Perhaps I should say 'more corrupt and subservient'.)

Hypocrisy

Western governments know about the corrupt practices universally necessary to carry out business in the areas involved, but they are not willing to leave their exports at a disadvantage. They may legislate one thing to pacify the idealists or competing nations, but what goes on behind the scenes is different.

Over many years, various pressure groups coerced a reluctant British government to investigate several huge arms deals involving a major British armaments supplier, in which corruption was alleged by aggrieved parties within the countries involved (in particular, Saudi Arabia and South Africa) and by competing arms suppliers. Eventually, prosecution was averted by accepting a plea bargain that involved no public disclosure of the evidence. The large size of the fines agreed upon can be taken as an indication of the magnitude of the corrupt pay-ments involved, running into many millions of pounds. It is interest-ing that there was no mention of even any thought being given to the interests of the taxpayers swindled in the countries in question. These were the ultimate victims. There was clearly only a desire to protect the corrupt rulers and thereby Protect British Interests. Undoubtedly, the matter was of great importance to the British economy. Many British jobs were at stake, and all political parties knew that silence was best.

Such hypocrisy is a fact of business and government. Of course it is denied; it is in itself a process of denial. More naïve and sanctimo-nious individuals practise hypocrisy by self-deception. It is so endemic in first-world democracies that political success is impossible without it. Consider for example the practice of agricultural subsidisation by

---

7   For more information see Moeletsi Mbeki, *Architects of Poverty*, Picador Africa, 2009 and Pan Macmillan South Africa.

countries that demand free trade. Hypocrisy is a universal phenomenon, a factor to be taken into account in any business strategy aimed at dealing with issues of corruption.

The examples given above should not be used to arrive at one-sided generalities about Britain or any other country. In most nations – including some African, Asian and Latin American nations in which overt corruption is rife – there are also movements and legislation to counter corruption, often headed by dedicated idealists. In Britain, at the same time that the government was suppressing the armaments scandal, strong new legislation was being introduced (and has since passed into law) under which entities suspected of bribery practically have to prove their innocence.

The political fallacy behind this unsatisfactory situation seems to derive from misplaced idealism on the part of Western governments, or rather, the electorate to which they answer. Such misguided (but well-meaning) idealists seek to impose their ethical aspirations on other countries – as unrealistic a notion as prohibition was in the USA. They are not addressing reality. They simply do not comprehend the difference between the personal ethical values shaped by generations of devout churchgoers (and confounded by hypocrites), and the attitudes of peoples for whom until recently 'the law' was an instrument of colonisation and exploitation and who found themselves criminalised by failure to adhere to unfair laws.

More stringent legislation and penalties only drive up the stakes for non-conformance, foster greater ingenuity in finding loopholes and produce more damaging brands of criminality. The realistic path would be to acknowledge that different countries have different characteristics, and not try to dictate the conduct of their internal affairs. The only parties that can establish and maintain a realistic anti-corruption policy are the government and legal establishment of the host country itself. In the absence of such understanding, the international project Executive is left with some difficult and uncertain choices, of the type where he may be 'damned if he does, and damned if he doesn't'.

These comments should not be interpreted as an invitation to abandon ethical principles, without which no organisation or nation can flourish. I'm saying only that we have to accept different values and practices in different societies, and structure our relationships accordingly.

The basic questions here include 'What is fair?' and 'What is fair competition?' Treatises can and have been written about these questions. There is an element of aggression in competition. Especially when the competition is introduced from outside a certain social group, the competitors may be seen as fair game for reprisal, by any means available. Personal relationships are essential to survival in less developed countries, and there is an expectation that business dealings will take these into account rather than resorting to 'fair competition'. Let me quote from the findings of experts in this field, Chabal & Daloz (Africa Works: Disorder as Political Instrument. James Currey, Oxford, 1999):

'What all African states share is a generalised system of patrimonialism and an acute degree of apparent disorder, as evidenced by a high level of governmental and administrative inefficiency, a lack of institutionalisation, a general disregard for the rules of the formal political and economic sectors, and a universal resort to personal(ised) and vertical solutions to societal problems.'

The Procedural Sub-committee
At the level of combating project piracy, the main problem is that the Board (or sometimes a cabal of its members) may be knowingly involved in practices in a foreign country that may be considered to be corrupt, but has to deny it. (I am tacitly assuming conformance to home country legislation, but there will still be many 'borderline' practices that it is not wise to disclose publicly.) It is a secret. And secrets create space for pirates, leading to internal corruption. Transactions may be made without adequate transparency. Payments without proper receipt. 'Commissions' paid out to 'agents' in shady fashion and with no real way of checking what backhanders and kickbacks took place.

What should the Director do about all this? Simply occupying the moral high ground is no solution. We are dealing with the real world here, not some idealised fantasy created for PR purposes or by sanctimonious political opportunists. In varying degree, corrupt practice involving foreign countries is widespread behaviour, shielded by appropriate PR and the bland lying that goes with it. The challenge for the Director is how to deal with unavoidable corrupt situations without incurring legal sanction or adverse media interest, and how to do this without compromising corporate oversight or promoting ethical rot within his own enterprise.

You may feel that I have a rather cavalier attitude towards the laws of certain countries. I have. In a really corrupt country, you will find laws and regulations that inherently conflict or are susceptible to arbitrary interpretation. Whatever you do, you are likely to infringe some regulations. That is their purpose: to make you a legitimate target who has to yield concessions (or simply pay) to avoid penalty. You can either accept that that is how business is here conducted, or go elsewhere. If you choose to stay, you will need a strategy to handle conduct within the host country and another to deal with the laws, lawyers, hypocrites and idealists in your own and associated countries. These strategies needs to be well thought out and be subject to stringent risk analysis and management.

The point made here is that the necessarily confidential practices involved have to be an addressable issue, if without record, between the Executive and the Director. If the enterprise operates on the basis of a nod and a wink, there will surely be many opportunities for pirates to exploit. There are also likely to be some poorly constructed 'deals', easily exposed by skilled investigators, and very difficult to defend, when a stringent risk process might have arrived at a safer and defensible methodology. These issues need to be controlled by a formal but poorly recorded process, for instance, a Board committee or sub-committee with a bland title like 'Ethics Committee' or 'Business Practices Sub-committee'. Or how about 'Procedural Sub-committee'? That could be practically anything.

The modern democratic state is a many-headed beast, and the heads can all bite in different directions simultaneously. It's unwise to disclose any controversial matters that don't have to be disclosed, and especially those issues which the ruling politicians don't, in truth, want to be disclosed. It's not just criminal investigation that has to be avoided. Both politicians and international businesses now live in a world of competitive hypocrisy, where disclosure of unwanted realities may be seen as a heaven-sent opportunity by competitors and opportunistic journalists. But the need for confidentiality shouldn't be allowed to result in sloppy practice.

13. Procurement and Contracts

Weakening of Competitive Processes
One of the main areas of piracy to look out for within projects is in the establishment of contracts – and especially large and expensive ones – to get the project work done. We shall address not the basics of contract law or the detailed methodology of drawing up contracts, but rather some of the shortcomings that can enrich the contractor or supplier at the expense of the Owner, and some by which the Owner simply loses opportunities and sustains losses because of inept or negligent performance by his own executives. We shall address not simple criminal practice, whereby a bribe might secure an order or a contract, but rather some more subtle issues.

The first question is whether sufficiently competitive processes are involved in selecting the contractor. This is not necessarily a simple issue: devious and sometimes unintentional means can be used to weaken competitive processes. The project charter (discussed later) to be approved at the outset of the project would be unacceptably incomplete without a procurement and contracting plan outlining how the best value will be obtained. Failure to build the project schedule around such a plan can stifle competitive procurement. For instance, it may be found, too late, that there is an inadequate balance between time spent on engineering, procurement and construction. Engineering and design may be performed to the entire satisfaction of some pirate engineers or architects, but over such a length of time that it may subsequently become necessary to abridge procurement procedures and construction time. Thus leaving insufficient time to negotiate the best procurement deals or use the most cost-effective construction practices, or even leading to that ultimate project disaster, chaos on the construction site. Value will be lost.

Failure to maintain a balance between the subsidiary goals of a project's specialists is a frequent cause of sub-optimal project performance. Consider the decline of a major international contractor that supplied technologically based processing plants to many industries. These were major and complex plants. The project management system veered towards the departmental style of management, the various process departments being regarded as the elite; after all, it was felt, this was where the corporation's competitive edge resided. A lead process engineer was assigned to each project. On a large project, this would be a prestigious individual with a plush office, next to the various technology directors. By contrast, the project manager (capital letters deliberately avoided!) shared an office with a few others, next to most of the project team, and had no such prestige. He could be, and frequently was, over-ruled in his decisions by the Technology Directorship. Any conflict between the requirements of the Process Department and the other project specialists tended to be resolved on the basis of process requirements, with little compromise. Cost and man-hour over-runs were inevitable. This once-powerful group had steadily declined over the years, to the mortification of its major shareholders, one of whom was heard to complain about the decline in value of advanced-technology process industries. He had no idea how much value was lost by that organisation's inability to structure its projects around a procurement and contracting plan.

In Chapters 3 and 4, we looked at several issues concerning the operational cost considerations arising from procurement decisions, and we will not revisit these save to remind the reader that appropriate policies must be included in the project procurement plan.

Probably the best means of knowing whether adequately competitive processes are being followed is by getting feedback from the market, in particular from competing suppliers and contractors whose bids were unsuccessful, or who declined to bid. It may not be necessary for the concerned Director to personally seek such feedback; it will suffice to verify that similar independent checks are in place to ensure effective competition. It is not enough to simply compare the winning bid with the budget – both may be inflated.

It may be, and too often is, found that there is no competitive procurement process, but that the contractor is appointed via a 'partnering' system. There is no way to ensure that the best value is obtained by such appointment, but there are usually several contractors who work very hard to establish such an arrangement. No need to wonder why.

All major contracts should be subjected to an in-depth risk analysis and risk management planning process, before a commitment is made. A detailed risk report should be available with a concise executive summary, exactly as per the Owner's overall project report already discussed in Chapters 1, 3 and 6. Once again, the complete definition of scope, quality, cost and time is essential, and without all four the contract will be unmanageable. A few important risks will be considered, but this is by no means exhaustive.

- Notwithstanding the comments above on competition, there may be good reason to exclude certain contractors from bidding – be careful not to pressurise the Project Manager in the wrong direction! Some contractors depend for their profits on making excessive and unreasonable claims for extra payment. The main way of countering this is of course to have a soundly drafted contract, and to manage it carefully. In particular, the Owner's manager needs to take care not to default on his own obligations, e.g. for provision of timely site access and provision of instructions such as drawings. But even with a sound contract and good management, a claim-orientated contractor will generate a lot of claims, which may be spurious but can bog down the Owner with litigation and uncertainty over a period of years. This 'uncertainty' can be damaging to the perceived worth of an enterprise or to the credibility of a government department.

  There are many tell-tale signs to detect such contractors; the best are their record of actual litigation and claims history on previous projects. It is usual for such a contractor to employ a 'claims consultant', as a matter of course, at the outset of a contract, maybe even as part of the negotiation team. Another sign is an apparently odd weighting of the breakdown of contract prices, for instance, over-pricing monthly site establishment charges and under-pricing rates per item of work – in preparation for an eventual claim for extended site establishment.

It is best to avoid such contractors if possible. Prequalification of contractors should include a good understanding of their attitude towards the generation of claims for extra payment and time extension, as evidenced by records of past contracts. Don't influence the Project Manager to get any contractor with a litigious record to bid.

- Every effort should be made to structure contracts to have payments based on outputs, not inputs. A 'man-hour',[8] or a construction equipment usage hour, is clearly an input that may vary greatly in its usefulness. Offers of service based on such input cost basis can hardly, if it all, be compared on any competitive basis. There may be little if any incentive for efficiency, and, worse, the contract effectively may become open-ended and produce runaway costs. I have witnessed (even participated in) contracts where a contractor – usually involved in consultancy or engineering or management services – is paid by a percentage of the direct cost of the project. This is insane. Where is the incentive to reduce the direct cost? You will find many consultants, in particular, who justify such practice as the 'professional norm'. It is – when dealing with weak clients. Of course, a consultant being paid a fixed fee can't be expected to do extra unpaid work to reduce overall costs; it may be wise to incentivise him to do so, after considering all the cautions on incentives previously mentioned.

As a final word of warning on this subject, there is a profession known as quantity surveyors. Naturally, they absolutely *love* to be paid for surveying quantities. For assistance in managing a rates-based contract, the Project Manager may very well require their services. But what if the quantity surveyor is engaged also to prepare the contracts, or even, *is* the Project

---

8   This most certainly includes, on an equal basis, 'woman-hours', but that is the customary term.

Manager? You can expect some rates-based contracts, where it would have been more effective to contract for the end product. Try to pay for the building, not for the bricks.

- Some Owners, and some managing contractors or consultants employed by Owners, fail to get good value from the market because of their own attitudes. And they're quite unable to see it, or maybe, as can be seen from the examples below, the Executive in charge is just too arrogant to care. The most cost-effective suppliers and contractors just don't want to do business with them.

This is best illustrated by example:

1. There's a mining group that we shall call Magnificent Metals. Its projects are all entrusted to a single individual heading a corporate department. He's called the 'Consulting Engineer' according to traditional practice, but his functions closely match those of an executive director. Mining is a tough business; that tends to extend from underground to the senior management. A very arrogant and tough individual occupied this position; we will call him Ivan the Terrible. Ivan had a greatly inflated opinion of his own knowledge and experience (which were, indeed, considerable, but partly outdated). He needed to employ engineering and management contractors for the larger projects, and always employed them on a 'man-hour' basis. This gave him the opportunity to dictate exactly how he wanted the man-hours to be utilised, and consequently the power to micro-manage all the project work, when he felt so inclined. Magnificent Metals' policies require that procurement be carried out on a competitive basis, but he often got around that by dictating to his contractors who their subcontractors should be. Needless to say, that enabled the subcontractors to operate very profitably. None of the better contractors wanted to work for Magnificent Metals. They would respond to requests for bids, but usually with inflated prices, happier to lose the contract than to put up with Ivan for only a modest reward. I won't elaborate any further. Magnificent Metals' mining developments

cost substantially more than their competitors' and suffered from a severe lack of innovation.

2. The contracting strategy at Martian Mining could hardly have been more different. They believed in rigorously controlled competitive bidding for their projects, buying the whole plant on a lump-sum basis in accordance with very detailed specifications. They were keen for contractors to use their ingenuity and initiative in order to offer the most cost-effective plant design and construction, but they were obsessed with the need, when assessing the bids received, to compare them all on the same footing. 'We must compare apples with apples,' they would say. So, although they requested bidders to offer their best 'fit for purpose' alternative to the base designs specified, each bidder was required to submit a bid also for the specified and detailed design case 'as a basis for comparative evaluation'. You can imagine the incentive to produce an alternative more cost-effective design! And when on occasion a bidder was sufficiently foolish to invest in the costly effort of offering a better design as an alternative, and Martian liked it, they might then reissue the enquiry based on the improved design, 'to be fair to all the bidders'. This actually happened a number of times; I am not making it up!

Procurement includes the exercise of power, the power to make decisions between competing parties. Both in managing the procurement process and in making the final choice of suppliers, executives wield power, which tends to corrupt the individual, or indeed a body of individuals. This corruption can generally be gauged by the attitude of the Executive and his procurement staff towards contractors and suppliers. Wise Owners should be supportive of and open to the entities on which his enterprise is ultimately dependent. All of the entities – not just country-club-cronies, whose subscriptions are likely paid by their employer, for good reason. Too often the Executive's attitude is rather superior or contemptuous, and there is a lack of close feedback from the whole supplying marketplace. In this case, you can be sure that substantial value is being lost to the Owner in the long run, even if there is no corruption involved, as legally defined.

Runaway Costs and Late Reporting
In Chapters 8 and 9, we considered projects where the eventual costs were way over budget but the cost reports failed to show this until far too late for any effective action to be taken. This doesn't necessarily constitute a disaster to the Owner, rather than a project delivery contractor, unless the Owner has contractually accepted responsibility for the runaway costs and the schedule delays that usually accompany them. One or more of three underlying causes is usually present:

1. Open-ended contracts. The project's contracts committed the Owner to pay on a basis of rates for items such as tons of steel to be fabricated and erected, and the quantities turned out to be far greater than expected. In some cases, the quantity estimation error was made out of apparent negligence, and the perpetrator, who was also the person charged with re-measurement as the project progressed, seemingly kept quiet to conceal the error. In other cases, the designers carried on with design work after the contract was signed, and simply didn't feel constrained to stay within the contract quantities and didn't report the changes. And many other types of undisclosed change were made, too complex and too boring (maybe too sad) to list. The consequences didn't properly find their way into the cost report until the contracts were being wound up after the final re-measurement of quantities.

2. Reverting to item 1(c) in Chapter 8: the budgeted work packages did not correspond to the way in which work was actually done. This mostly happens in rates-based pipework, structural steel or electrical reticulation contracts, if the control budget is based on quantities of each type of piping component or mass of steelwork, without breakdown into individual drawings. The costs being incurred cannot be properly compared with the budget until the total project design or construction is nearly completed.

3. Failure to restrict or evaluate potential or actual contractual claims. Sometimes this can originate in the project's engineering and management office, but more often it happens at the construction site, when the Owner's supervisor either lacks

commercial acumen or is negligent in the control of changes. A variety of changes and impacts may be involved:

- late design changes
- rework necessitated by design errors, including those which are fantasies created by the construction workers
- unexpected underground conditions
- delays caused by third parties or weather
- failure to supply promised information or services to the contractor on time
- interference with the contractor's work by other contractors. Some of the resulting cost increases may be delayed until well after the contract's completion, depending on the claims evaluation and settlement process.

In all these cases, the need for more effective oversight should be apparent. There may have been systems within the projects that were supposed to prevent such happenings, but they just weren't functional.

The need to realistically address risks that may impinge on the contractor's performance at the Owner's cost requires further emphasis. We have already addressed force majeure and the 'fringe' issues around that, and risk management in general. The point to emphasise here is that when risks such as those mentioned in item 3 above exist, risk mitigation measures should include ensuring that if the risk does materialise, the contract does not become open-ended because the possible need to deal with the consequences was excluded from the contract scope and pricing schedules. Contract conditions generally require that, in the event of extra work required by unforeseen circumstances, there is an onus on the contractor to minimise extra costs that the Owner may incur, but this is usually rather difficult to manage, and especially so if the contract conditions allow generous rates for any extra work. If the prescient Owner is able to negotiate contract conditions in which the contractor shares some of the adverse consequences of unforeseen extra work, there is a built-in mechanism to minimise the additional work and to promote its efficient performance.

In some instances of very late reporting of runaway costs, the projects may have been of the type where an unachievable target had been set in the first place, to make the project look more attractive. Perhaps this may have been no coincidence. Maybe a Board which starts off a project by deluding itself – or, worse, deliberately misleading the shareholders, including those who want to be misled – sets the organisational tone that is followed by such failure in management. Perhaps in such cases delayed cost reporting may not have been caused by negligence alone; there might have been some management direction involved, with the specific purpose of delaying the bad news.

In relation to procurement, the Executive, Owner or politician seeking the go-ahead for an unaffordable project has a choice of three main abuses. The first, as we saw in previous chapters, is to somehow arrive at an unreasonably low cost estimate. The second is to disregard or understate contractual and pricing risks. The third, which is a hybrid of the previous two, is effectively to by-pass the estimating work, by entering into a pre-project contract to perform the project work at an unrealistically low price, which the contractor is happy to accept because he knows that his price can and will be substantially increased because of contractual flaws. I believe that this is the most dangerous deception in the present context.

14. Sub-contracts

Sub-contractor Preference and Nomination

In the previous chapter, we touched on the behaviour of Ivan the Terrible, who dictated the sub-contractors to be employed by his main contractors, thereby defeating to some extent the forces of competitive procurement process. He also weakened the management ability of his main contractors: the sub-contractors were well aware of Ivan's patronage and disinclined to strictly follow the requirements of their putative direct employer. Result: higher overall cost, lower efficiency.

Mismanagement through interference with sub-contractor employment is a device so commonly employed by pirates that it is worth special mention. The nomination of suppliers or specified brands is a very similar device, which I consider to be a subset of the case of nominating a sub-contractor. As I write this I feel almost apologetic that such obvious issues should need to be mentioned at all – and yet this form of abuse is widespread and exists to some degree in most countries.

As a main contractor is (by definition) appointed by or on behalf of the Owner, the potential abuse of the practice of sub-contractor nomination invariably involves the Owner's organisation, as in the case of Ivan. Here are some typical reasons used to justify the practice:

- To standardise proprietary components or software, typically electrical, instrumentation and machine components, so that spare parts inventory and maintenance training may be reduced within a particular enterprise or works.

- To ensure that work performed and items supplied under a critical sub-contract will be carried out satisfactorily.
- To facilitate local participation in an international project. This is often a politically-dictated requirement in developing countries.
- To attempt to improve efficiency on a construction site, by reducing the number of sub-contractors offering a common service to the main contractors.

The first issue, standardisation, is necessary for most industrial plants. The potential negative procurement consequences can only be controlled by the Owner, rather than at main contractor level. The Owner should first identify those proprietary items which are so commonly available from different sources that competitive purchase is available – these items usually require no action. Then there are those items which may practically only be available from a single source or a small number of possibly collusive sources. The identity of such items is apt to vary between different countries – there may be a single importer, protected from competition by a sole agency agreement or by local government trade restrictions. If the Owner is convinced of a need to standardise on such items, he must first in best-value fashion set up a long-term purchase agreement (known as a 'frame order') with the supplier. He must ensure that exactly the same terms (or better) are available to any main contractor who may be compelled to purchase the items. Alternatively, he could set up an agreement by which a commission is payable to the Owner on purchases made by the main contractor. This practice is liable to abuse, and is not recommended unless required in pursuit of a transfer-pricing strategy, which will be addressed in Chapter 19.

The same considerations apply to the second case listed above; the full deal has to be struck between the Owner and the proposed sub-contractor, not left to a main contractor who will have no purchasing leverage. The Owner should carefully consider whether such nominated sub-contracts are really necessary, as they easily give rise to claims by the main contractor. It is normal that the main contract will include the right of approval or veto of sub-contractors. Especially if this right is diligently exercised up front, before the main contract has been awarded, vulnerability to later claims may be greatly reduced. Even if exercised later, critical overview of the sub-contractor selection process is recommended, to ensure that the process is conducted according to the Owner's best long-term interests.

We have touched on the formal ways of getting a preferred sub-contractor, but there are also informal ways, as practised by Ivan the Terrible. Engineering contracts for the design of mines usually have a sizeable electrical and instrumentation (E & I) portion. Ivan liked to have this work carried out by the good firm of Sparks & Muchavoc. Perhaps it was no coincidence that Lenny Sparks was Ivan's frequent golf partner, and Mika Muchavoc was married to Ivan's niece. Ivan wouldn't dream of suggesting to a potential main contractor that Sparks & Muchavoc should be employed as E & I sub-contractors, and, besides, this was contrary to Magnificent's 'ethical practices'. The most he would ever overtly do was that, if he was asked by new potential main contractors about required standards for E&I work performance, he might inform them that 'a lot of our E&I work is done by Sparks & Muchavoc; perhaps you should speak to them'. No nudge, no wink, but they usually got the message.

Occasionally a contractor would try to buck the trend. Brian Scout, Chief Engineer of Simply Serious Engineers (SSE), hated working with Sparks & Muchavoc as sub-contractors. In a tender to Magnificent Metals, he insisted on including his own in-house E&I engineers. SSE were in due course called in for technical review of the tender, and were duly grilled by Ivan, with no mention whatever of Sparks & Muchavoc. 'Look at your instrument guy's CV,' he said to Scout. ' Buttercup University, good God! And all this work in the food industry! Are we going to have mines looking like ice-cream factories?' He also tore into the SSE E&I engineering procedures, and some previous projects that were rather unsuccessful. Ivan was a master of destructive criticism. 'Come back in a couple of days with some better ideas,' he said. 'We'll give you one last chance.'

SSE's Marketing Manager, Will Friendly, had a target to meet, and this was defined by the value of contracts awarded to SSE, without deduction for any work sub-contracted. Speaking to Scout in the Library Hotel bar after the meeting, he pulled no punches. 'We were mauled, Brian. That was ugly. Stop being so arrogant and Give the Customer

What He Wants.' Scout nodded glumly, and after a few more drinks was ready to telephone 'bloody Sparky', who was expecting the call.

Turning to the third example of sub-contractor nomination, 'facilitation of local participation' embraces a monstrous legion of corrupt practice. It is sometimes the avenue for a bribe, in particular through a party who has a financial interest in the favoured local organisations. This can backfire, and, anyway, when a corrupt deal is struck, all sorts of worrying crocodiles are likely to appear, as outlined in Chapter 12. Whatever agreements are made under this heading require stringent independent overview.

The final case listed above, nomination of a single sub-contractor to service a number of main contractors, should only be considered in remote sites where the provision of such services is very limited. Such practice should be subject to the same Owner obligations as mentioned for the first two cases. In addition some special difficulties arise. These include the multiplicity of contractual claims the Owner is likely to face when the service is inadequate or priorities have to be set on service provision. The best strategy in remote sites is usually to stick with one overall main contractor who is responsible for all the services required. Alternatively, establish the service as a separate organisation, but don't enforce its use or mention it at all in the contracts.

As a much more general observation, the Director should be sceptical about all seemingly unnecessary or questionable decisions that contractually fragment the work of a project. So often this is done as an exercise of power and patronage – possibly with some 'backhanders' involved – rather than out of acceptable practice of seeking overall better value.

15. Contracting out Operational Services and Privatisation

Contracting out Services

In Chapter 3, we discussed how project definition and the required capital outlay can be substantially affected by the decision on whether or not to outsource some of the services and resources needed for post-project operation. We noted the importance of probing and exactly defining such decisions for the purpose of properly setting project targets. It is almost inevitable that a decision will be taken that some services – a few of the usual are addressed below – be contracted out. This opens opportunities for pirates which will now be examined at greater length. All of these opportunities need to be probed at the pre-project stage. Once a project has been authorised with an assumption (sometimes implicit) that certain services or needs will be contracted out, it may already be too late to prevent pirates from extracting gains that should rather be garnered by the investing enterprise. The pirates' gains may remain as thorns in the side of the enterprise in the long term.

The fundamental issue behind this necessary scrutiny is one of competition: is there going to be real competition to provide the services? Even if there is, might a cartel or monopoly develop in the future?

The first concern to be addressed is the tenure of land or property, which is usually a basic requirement for a large new enterprise or facility. Even though impersonal, this need should be regarded as an essential service, and often a service behind services provided by project and operational contractors, with a limited supply available. Few Boards would authorise a major construction project without securing the rights for whatever land is directly required for the construction and operation of the facility being created. Sometimes, though, insufficient attention is given to all the land that will be required – for personnel accommodation, for service suppliers, for waste disposal, for construction contractors and for the future. If this indirectly required land is not secured by the Owner before project go-ahead, it is likely to become more expensive. It is not unusual to see property developers making fortunes in the wake of a large project. In the long run, those fortunes will amount to extra cost for the enterprise (or the taxpayer, in the case of a government project). Pre-project attention should be given as per any other major future cost or lateral opportunity.

The next most usual issue is maintenance services and spare parts. Any supply dependency during future operation which may be created by a project procurement decision needs careful examination, in keeping with the magnitude of its potential cost. Machinery items in particular may be subject to inadequate and over-expensive service and spare part provision, especially but not only when purchased from the cheapest source. Some suppliers reckon to make all their profits from after-sales income, and will offer their machines at a discount. They can increase their after-sales income in a number of ways apart from those already mentioned: by specifying over-stringent service needs, by built-in obsolescence, by unreasonable imposition of intellectual property rights over local manufacture of spare parts. Understanding and countering such practices involves a lot of hard work at the pre-project and project stage. This will not be done effectively by a project team not properly charged to do it, and especially not by a project Executive or manager incentivised only on a basis of lowest project cost and earliest completion.

Any unique technology required for future operations and custom operational software can also lead to expensive dependencies. The latter will be addressed in Chapter 18.

Further items for consideration include the purchase of major operational supplies, transport of all kinds (supply, product delivery, personnel), hotel accommodation and the consequences of any particular local regulations or circumstances that will effectively restrict competition among suppliers. Substantial exercise of due diligence is needed here, and oversight is required to ensure that it is done properly. It usually isn't.

Privatisation

The transfer of government services or assets to the private sector is a special case of contracting out services, and is worthy of some special attention.

To lead into this, consider the outcome of a recent enquiry into the collapse of the consortium that took over a large government service, which will not be identified. The transfer of the service to private enterprise was to be accompanied by major construction work required to upgrade the service. The enquiry panel included a Leading Engineer, who noted that a principal member of the consortium was a construction contractor to whom the consortium had awarded all the construction work without any competitive tendering process. Presumably, the contractor had made a profit out of this contract before the consortium went under. The Leading Engineer described the contractor-cum-consortium-member's conduct as 'immoral'.

I was quite shaken by the Leading Engineer's naivety. What did he think the construction contractor was doing as part of a consortium to provide a service that was not his business? It's natural for a contractor to try to develop opportunities where he will not have to compete, not have to cut his price to the bone, not have to assume risks. Incredible to blame the contractor, rather than the politicians and the bureaucrats who allowed the non-competitive opportunity to be created.

On the Executive's side, an underlying piracy issue arising out of the contracting-out of services, including privatisation, is often that there is a short-term financial gain to the outsourcer or privatiser. Finances may appear to be rosier – for a while. Enough time to make project performance look better at the immediate post-project evaluation. Enough time to win an election.

Here are two major piracy issues, and therefore careful oversight must be exercised. The following are a few of the questions to be pursued:

- Will there be real and long-term competition to provide the services being outsourced or privatised? If not, how do we prevent the end-user from being screwed?
- Are any of the short-term suppliers or contractors to a proposed privatised entity in any way tied to the entity?
- What internal and external safeguards will exist to keep the entity efficient? This becomes very important if, as is often the case, an entity without direct competition such as a toll road, a transport system or a public utility ends up receiving price adjustment based on input costs.
- Has the Owner performed a really stringent financial analysis of the proposed outsourcing or privatisation, based on NPV or IRR, and does this tie in with the long-term financial policies of the Owner? To be clear: for an NPV comparison a spreadsheet should be built up of the future costs to the user, and the discounted present value should be compared with the proceeds of privatisation. When building up the future-costs-to-user spreadsheet, for each significant item the question must be asked, 'What mechanism exists to contain the cost at that value?'
- Has a thorough risk management process been conducted by the Owner's Executive? Is the report available for scrutiny?
- Who stands to gain here? And will the happy recipients of this gain have earned it? Has any undue influence been exerted?

Please don't infer from the above that I am opposed to outsourcing or privatisation on principle – only to its abuse, which usually derives from the creation of anti-competitive opportunities or the understatement of long-term costs. Where the reverse is the case and proper technical, financial and risk analysis has been performed, I believe that outsourcing and privatisation are good for the enterprise and for the economy as a whole.

16. Lateral Opportunities and Owner-Contractor Relationships

At Its Simplest: Paying by Business Improvement

Just as the development of a business inevitably includes reviews and plans to 'sweat the assets', so should the development of a project. Many organisations fail to do this adequately. Consider the following as a simple example of how this may come about.

Various merchants, and in particular those providing management consultancy and software services, sometimes want to do business on the basis of payment in accordance with measured business improvement. Two observations on this apparent possibility for money to be grown on trees:

- All the precepts of incentivation, as mentioned in Chapter 1, should apply, just as they would to any company executive. The failure to satisfy any of these precepts is likely an indication of piracy.
- It is usually very difficult to isolate the multiple causes and effects relating to the success or failure of a business. The deal can often only be meaningful if the entire business or division of the business is run within constraints required by the business improver.

In further consideration of the above, there is evidently at least one additional economy that may be made by the Board of a company entering into such a deal. Fire the chief executive and executives responsible, as their services will no longer be relevant! Of course, this may be considered a little harsh in the case of an organisation that is strapped for cash and is thus incapable of making the improvements any other way.

Sub-contracting the Challenge

The foregoing example is the simplest form of a wider issue relating to how the Executive responds to major perceived project challenges, including both threats and opportunities. In previous chapters we addressed mainly the Executive issues arising out of project definition and target-setting. There are also inevitably opportunities for the Executive to pass on perceived challenges to third parties. This may be done in a way that is consistent with the Owner's best interests, but it may also lead to the unreasonable enrichment of third parties, while the Owner's Executive enjoys the benefits that may ensue without much effort or risk to himself.

I am not advocating the practice of retaining Executive responsibility for the direct performance of all project functions, but rather reminding the reader that a prime role of the Executive is to strategise the project's execution in accordance with the long-term needs of the Owner, including:

- retaining direct responsibility for, and developing internal capability for key strategic functions of the enterprise or government department;
- outsourcing non-core functions to the extent that competitive suppliers and contractors are available, and in a fashion whereby best value is obtained;
- avoiding the loss of key technology and associated development opportunities to contractors or to third parties such as consultants, who may then assist competitors. ('Don't breed your own competition.')

Failure to do this properly often manifests itself as the wholesale transfer of responsibility to a single consultant or managing contractor, or the acceptance of 'deals' which are offered in a way that by-passes effective competition, often with an apparently inviting finance package included. It is usually possible for a diligent Owner's Executive to arrive at a much better conclusion, without the negative aspects of losing control of the project and failing to develop the Owner's project capabilities. There is no golden rule to be followed here; it is natural that a capable contractor will wish to grow his business at the expense of the Owner, but it is equally incumbent on the Owner's Executive to try to achieve the opposite.

Relationships with Service Providers

There are three main ways for the Executive to get project work done:

1. Direct employment (or 'hire') and management of resources.
2. Contracting of work in packages, using the process of competition to obtain best value.
3. Negotiating 'deals' with parties such as consultants and contractors. This includes 'relationships' that are non-competitive by nature and are generally intended to be symbiotic.

A small or emergent 'start-up' enterprise tends to be driven towards the third method, through initial unwillingness to directly employ non-core resources, and lack of capability and confidence to manage a competitive process at the higher levels. Indeed, project financiers may require the wholesale entrustment of a project to an established contractor, to give credence to the aspirations of an emergent enterprise. But the larger or better-established the enterprise or government department, the less should it need to rely on such relationships, which inevitably carry some negative aspects as outlined here and in previous chapters.

Common examples of abuse that arises from poorly structured Owner/contactor relationships are:

• Government ministers or senior civil servants who leave and take up highly remunerative roles in private-sector organisations with which their departments enjoy non-competitive (type 3) relationships.

- Project executives and department managers who go on to form companies providing services to both their former employers and, more dangerously, to competitors.

In both cases, the pirates usually commence their strategies well before leaving the organisation.

These are important and widespread organisational issues requiring close monitoring on behalf of the Owner. The soundest way to avoid abuses of type 3 relationships is to prohibit them wherever possible.

Over-Oversight

It should be noted in this context that all project oversight, and typically of a project contractor by an Owner's Executive, can be taken too far. After demotivating his contractors by fragmenting their project teams with the imposition of various unmanageable sub-contractors, that master of project piracy, Ivan the Terrible, would finish off the demolition job by imposing on his contractors a large team of Owner's engineers. These were charged with questioning and second-guessing every action of the contractor's team. In a narrative mainly directed at emphasising the need for project oversight, it is time to call attention to the possibility that oversight can be taken too far. Much too far.

No project team is going to give their best performance if they are continually diverted by the requirement to satisfy the whims of over-viewers who themselves have no responsibility for timely and economic completion of the work.

17. A Tilt at Windmills

Wrongly Quantified Green Thinking

'Renewable energy' projects currently receive much attention and lend themselves to a peculiar type of abuse. Before addressing the projects, let's explore the mindset that inspires them. This unfortunately brings us into the realm of politics; but when politicians become government ministers they become both Executives and Directors, and need to be watched over accordingly.

The use of superficially attractive ideals is a cornerstone of political manipulation. Sometimes deliberate manipulation is even unnecessary: people delude themselves, or have become deluded by their education (or lack thereof), and politicians take advantage. One of the recurring features of these superficial ideals is a lack of proper quantification. The start of this process is usually failure to count the cost of a proposed action; sometimes not to count it properly, sometimes not to count it at all, because the benefits are held to be self-evident. This can be put another way – a failure to address the negative implications, which can often far outweigh the good intentions.

I call the mindset applicable to the examples that follow 'wrongly quantified Green thinking', relating to the colour and the political ideology, not to a person. The emphasis here is on the quantification process, and not on the underlying ideals of Green politics. These seem to be laudable, if often unachievable because of over-population, which it is not politic to address. The aspect of Green thinking challenged here is the over-simplistic consideration of major environmental issues, which are too readily and too frequently approached in an emotive rather than scientific fashion. Please note that I am not questioning the need for active environmental conservation; this is surely critically important in a world that is falling apart before the forces of unprincipled greed. I am questioning the way that the processes and the goals are sometimes formulated. Good intentions and golden visions are not in themselves enough to justify and define expensive projects.

As a small but simple illustration of my concerns, consider the case of the offshore oil platform whose useful life had ended. The owners calculated the cost and residual value of towing it to a suitable location for dismantling and conversion into steel scrap. They then compared the cost of sinking it in situ, and they found this to be the most economical solution. They also evaluated the environmental consequences, in particular the danger to navigation and the impact of pollution, and regarded these as acceptable. A small quantity of residual oil could not be prevented from washing into the sea. The quantity was held to be well within the capability of destruction by natural biological processes before any oil could reach any sensitive area. When the plan for sinking the rig was publicised, there was an outcry from Europe's Green movement. Their attack focused on the effects of pollution by residual oil to be released into the sea, and their 'experts' calculated and trumpeted a value for the quantity of oil, held to constitute a potential ecological disaster. The rig owners produced their own detailed calculations for inspection, and the Greens were eventually forced to concede that their quantity calculation was far too high. Way out. Did this stop them? Not a bit of it! Political pressure was reinforced, now on the basis that, 'Well, any pollution at all is unacceptable.' The rig owners were eventually compelled to tow the rig away, and a lot of money and resources were wasted that could otherwise have been put to productive economic purpose.

Renewable Energy
As a rather more complex issue for some, because of its technical basis, consider 'renewable energy', one of the everlasting aspirations of Green ambition. A subject with a name like this starts off on a bad

footing, which probably augurs some of the nonsense ahead. A basic tenet of non-nuclear physics is that energy can neither be created nor destroyed; energy is never lost, there is no reason to renew it. What these fellows evidently want to address is 'renewable resources for the generation of power', and in particular electrical power. The difference is not semantic; there is a major difference between power and energy, and this is at the root of some misguided policies. Energy is mainly latent, whereas power is an entity that can be either present or absent at a given instant. Energy has many forms, such as heat and work, which are interchangeable, subject to certain restrictions. Electrical energy is a form of work energy, which implies that it can be used, 100%, for purposes such as moving objects. Power is the rate of producing work energy; machines used for the production of electrical energy are rated by power output.

One of the basic limitations of the production of electrical energy is that it is very expensive to store. The method of large-scale storage found to be the most economical in most locations is the pumped storage scheme, where water is pumped from a lower reservoir to an upper reservoir, and then can generate power very quickly when required, by flowing back down through a turbine. Such systems are very expensive to build, and the overall efficiency of power delivered divided by power consumed is unlikely to exceed 70%, and may be as low as 50%. So, for the most part, power must be generated when it is consumed. Little more power can be delivered than the primary generating capacity available at the instant that the power is demanded.

Let's consider wind power, one of the perennial favourites of the Greens. It comes with the obvious major limitation of no wind, no power. The viability totally depends on the frequency of good steady winds. Windmills have been and still are widely used, especially in less developed regions, to pump water out of the ground on a small scale. The water can be stored in an elevated tank: it doesn't have to be used when it is pumped up. But unfortunately electricity doesn't work the same way. To each unit, to each kilowatt-hour of energy generated must be ascribed a value based not only on the quantity generated but also on the time of generation, including length of time, predictability and consistency, and how these match the demands of the users.

Conventional evaluation of wind power economics is often made on a basis of energy value alone. Even on this grossly inadequate basis, it is seldom economic, and can only be introduced with subsidies. For sure, there are exceptions: remote localities, endlessly windy places, where wind-based power generation is appropriate. But most people live in more pleasant climes. To satisfy the base-loads of most countries, wind power generation is only good for the windmill salesmen, and probably also for certain politicians who facilitate their subsidies. The subsidy is often hidden; consider the case, as in many parts of Europe, where electrical power distributors are obliged to buy wind-generated power as and when it is available. To operate in a fashion whereby this power input can be accommodated requires expensive power storage or standby generating devices that add greatly to overall system cost and diminish overall efficiency. The costs thus incurred can amount to a subsidy of anything up to 300% on the apparent cost of wind power, in addition to any subsidies on capital cost.

Global Warming

A blanket subsidy is the very worst form of project incentive; it is not windmills per se that are needed. To arrive at an optimal socio-economic outcome, the governments in question need to start with a clear idea of the ultimate objective, and attempt to quantify it. The ultimate objective seems to be the reduction of global warming, a measured phenomenon which is seen as being probably very damaging to the environment and the economy. Some correlation has been noted between the measured carbon dioxide concentration in the global atmosphere and the mean ambient temperature. There is some controversy as to whether the correlation corresponds to a causal relationship whereby carbon dioxide concentration causes increased temperature. Alternatively, increased temperature (following meteorological events that are not properly understood) may cause increased carbon dioxide concentration, e.g. through reduced solubility in water; or the interaction may be more complex. Although clearly highly desirable, it is not essential to establish certain knowledge. If considerable numbers of scientific experts are convinced that the underlying cause of global warming is excessive carbon emissions, and that the ultimate consequences may be quantified as catastrophic, then until and unless this possible scenario can be *proved to be incorrect*, there is a known grave risk that must be mitigated.

Leaving aside the difficulties in implementation, the only real downsides to the reduction of carbon emissions seem to be classifiable as economic, and quantifiable in financial terms. Thus the sensible way to go about the reduction is the tax on emissions, and use of the revenue from the taxation to mitigate the consequent economic hardships arising out of the increased cost and lower availability of power. The tax should be increased until the optimum outcome is reached. This is not the practical extinction of carbon emissions, but the point at which the marginal reduction of (financially assessed) Risk of climatic catastrophe is equal to the corresponding marginal increase of cost of emissions reduction. It may well be found to be close to the point at which the cost of the emissions reduction is equal to the remaining assessed Risk after the measures are taken.

Logically, carbon credits should also be awarded for measures which reduce atmospheric carbon dioxide. For instance, instead of moaning about deforestation, use a calculated amount of the taxes on carbon emissions to pay for the maintenance of the forests.

In conclusion, the right way to set a level playing field for competition between fossil-fuel-generated power and power from renewable resources is to penalise the former in proportion to the perceived environmental damage. If projects to supply windmills flourish under such a taxation regime and without any subsidies (direct or indirect), then they should be considered to be a benefit. But otherwise, please regard them as an abomination.

18. The Real Software Pirates

Pitfalls in the Procurement of Business Management Systems

Electronic computers have, in recent years, proved to be enormously useful devices for the operation of almost everything, including all forms of administration relating to the management of enterprises and government departments. The rapid increase of applications has developed an insufficiently critical mindset in many users. They tend to buy computer applications – essentially the software – in a way that they wouldn't dream of doing for any traditional purchase such as a steam engine.

We are not addressing standard PC applications here; standard PC software is regarded as a consumer rather than a project issue, and although abuses may be enormous, that is not within our present ambit.

We are addressing enterprise and government management software, and the project of purchasing the software and getting it operational. In particular, the sort of software used for management reporting, financial control, control of large projects, integration of engineering work, control of government departments; big, complex programs or suites of programs. These will be collectively described as business management systems (BMS). No real software supplier names or brands will be mentioned!

Perhaps it will be easiest to outline where purchasers go wrong by outlining a typical project. The executives of a large enterprise, let's call it Mainly Manufacturing (MM), were aware of a degree of chaos in their organisation. There invariably is, in organisations that are not yet fossilised and obsolescent. But being executives, and several floors above the day-to-day activities, they felt more vulnerable about incidents of chaos than the workers who were closer to the action. When the occasional 'Oh shit!' incident came to light, they worried about what might happen next. What else might be out of control? Could anyone be trusted? Surely the enterprise could be run more efficiently than this? This is fertile ground for the software salesman.

Mainly Manufacturing were aware that some of their competitors were well ahead in the race to computerise operations. They were aware of the favoured BMS being used by large corporations. But they didn't know much about how to go about choosing one. They thought their own head of IT wasn't experienced enough to be entrusted with managing the proposed software project, and headhunted a new overall manager, Freddy Freek. Freek was an experienced systems analyst, but unfortunately, he had very little experience of factory administration. He also had minimal commercial acumen, a limitation common in IT experts. He came with his own strong preferences in software, but realised that he had to take the executives through a software selection process, or they'd feel cheated of the exercise of executive choice.

Freek began by trying to understand the management processes at MM. He assembled a team of aspiring young managers seconded from MM's main departments, and together they prepared a specification of what the software must do, which included practically every business process. The existing business processes were to be supplemented by many improvements that computerisation seemed to make possible. In particular, many new controls were added to satisfy the concerns of the top executives. Not surprisingly, the aspiring managers saw an opportunity to build up unassailable positions for themselves as the knowledgeable individuals holding the key to complex future operations. Or so they thought.

As required by MM's procurement policies, Freek consulted with the Head of Procurement, Hop, on how to go about the procurement process for the software. Hop was most unhappy to learn that the characteristics of the BMS available were so different that they couldn't be

directly compared on price. Freek put it like this: 'We issue our specifications and conditions of purchase, and ask the shortlisted suppliers
to give us a presentation on what they can offer. Then we calculate the
value each competing BMS should bring to our business, compare this
with the suppliers' cost estimates, and choose.'

'That's all wrong,' said Hop. 'We need the tenderers to come up
with promises of what they will do for our business, so we can hold
them to their promises. And what do you mean by cost *estimate*? We
require a firm price.'

With an exasperated sigh, Freek replied, 'We're not buying some
stupid steam engine here! This is a very complex management system.
We know our business' (he meant, the corporate we, not himself) 'and
they don't. There's no way the tenderers can commit to any kind of
meaningful promise of final business results. Are we going to get real
here, or carry on with stone-age management systems?'

Reluctantly, and not wanting (along with many other executives) to
be a stone-age relic, Hop was drawn into the plan. Presentations were
made, assessments were performed, contractual negotiations were held
and eventually a contract with Shaftem Software Systems (SSS) was
signed. Hop and his team failed to appreciate the consequences of some
important contractual issues on which SSS insisted. For instance, being
more used to purchasing proprietary hardware articles than custom software, they saw nothing unreasonable in agreeing that all the intellectual property of the software remained SSS property, without limitation.
Freek understood the possible consequences, but he was too commercially naïve to understand that a better deal might be had if that's what
it took for SSS to get the order. He kept silent on this and similar issues
by which his commercial colleagues may have secured a better deal, if
they had his technical experience regarding what could go wrong. He
was keen to work with the SSS professionals, and didn't at all relate to
their commercial managers smiling in the background, or in truth, to his
own commercial team.

A joint MM–SSS project team was assembled, under the management of an MM executive, to carry out the new BMS project. The full
details of this corporate catastrophe will not be described. Nor will we
address the age-old project problem of whether the failure of this project
was caused by mismanagement, or whether the project team was headed

for inevitable disaster because of shortcomings of the pre-project work and the deal that was entered into. The worst outcomes included:

- The implementation budget was exceeded by 400%.
- The BMS roll-out was six months behind schedule.
- The roll-out was chaotic, and it took several more months before the BMS was working, after a fashion. There were severe production control, inventory control and accounting problems, which haven't been sorted out satisfactorily to this day. Frequently, operations were hamstrung by the new controls. Data formatting and inputs had to be 100% correct, or systems ground to a halt. Severe losses were sustained because of the chaos, which SSS ascribed variously to 'system specification errors', 'finger trouble' (meaning careless data input by MM staff) and 'resistance to change'.
- To this day, MM have to employ several highly expensive SSS consultants full-time to solve system problems as they arise. MM dare not terminate the agreement with SSS, whose rates rise significantly each year. They are completely dependent on SSS to prevent their systems from collapsing.
- MM have recently learned that the software improvements developed at great expense to them are now on sale to their competitors. They are, after all, SSS's intellectual property.
- SSS shares continue to rise; MM's have plummeted.

Conclusions
These are left entirely to the reader.

19. Transfer Pricing and Specific Taxation Issues

Over- and Under-invoicing

In a global entity, transfer pricing is usually a major issue, and its optimal management can be one of the most important factors of company profitability. Generally, the most important considerations are taxation and the ability to move financial assets from a country of origin to an offshore haven. To the extent that the enterprise is able to determine under which national jurisdiction profit is taken, and how funds are channelled, the opportunity arises to minimise taxation. National governments and organisations such as the Organisation for Economic Co-operation and Development (OECD) are well aware of this, and devise regulations and various forms of oversight to extract the maximum taxation without driving the taxpayers away.

In the case of commodities, under normal circumstances there is not much opportunity for under-invoicing their export from the country of origin. The international markets are well and publicly documented, on a daily basis. There are some exceptions where transfer gains are to be had – it has been noted that oil tankers travel much more slowly when the oil price is rising than when it is decreasing. In times of rapid rise, extra tankers are practically unavailable for hire.

In the case of manufactured goods, under-invoicing is often more difficult to detect, but generally there is sufficient competition from low-cost manufacturing centres to make this unnecessary. The main gains are to be had in the intermediate transactions taking place between export from low-cost country of origin A and ultimate import into high-price market destination B. There may be an intermediate, entirely nominal but very profitable transaction in and out of a tax haven, or an actual physical trans-shipment with possible repackaging or reassembly. Provision of exported services is an even more juicy market for the transfer-pricing profiteer, very hard to detect if handled carefully.

Projects that incorporate imports and inputs from global sources present opportunities for the transfer price manipulator. It is very difficult for a government agency to accurately verify the pricing of items such as custom-built machinery and specialist services, which may range from engineering and management services to the performance of construction contracts. And, yes, our software salesmen are out there in the thick of it.

There are many ways for a project Owner to exercise transfer price manipulation. The most advantageous methods vary from country to country, and change with time as politicians and their taxmen get smarter (as they see it) or greedier (as the trading enterprises see it). Two of the main methods are:

- Trading through a third party controlled by the Owner, even a string of third parties in appropriate locations, to gain benefits as outlined below, and
- A 'commission' paid by an exporter in country A, in one way or other, to the Owner. The goods or services are then sold to the Owner's receiving project entity in country B at a price inflated by the amount of the commission. The commission may be dressed up in several ways, for instance as a 'licence fee' for the inclusion of special technology, or as a 'group discount', etc.

Opportunities and Challenges for Globalised Owners and Contractors

The usual objective of project transfer pricing manipulation is to make the project appear to be more expensive than it really is, in the country where the investment is made. The Owner's possible gains from such practice include:

- Reducing taxation. In countries where taxation is based on the profit arising from the investment rather than on the revenue, less taxes may be paid if the depreciation is taken on the greater value arising from artificially inflated project cost. There may also be tax breaks in the form of rapid depreciation allowed on book value. Of course, the gains in taxation of the operating enterprise have to be balanced against any additional customs duties or VAT.
- Gaining some extra leverage out of project subsidies or low-rate bank loans.
- Transferring funds from a destination where there are exchange controls. This is unlikely to be used in an initial project, but might be used for an upgrade paid for out of operating revenue. Importing over-expensive custom software is ideal for this purpose; the offshore 'backhander' to the Owner is easily dressed up as an entirely separate intellectual property fee, nothing at all to do with the project.
- Accumulating funds in an intermediate tax haven.
- Inflating the value of a share in a joint venture, e.g. with a host-country government agency.

Similar devices and potential gains are available to international project execution contractors. There are many practices that are considered to be and some that actually are illegal, depending on the legal environments involved. This may raise severe concerns for the project professionals involved: are their employer's requirements legal? Few project professionals would wish to risk spending time in jail, especially in a third-world country.

Back to the Procedural Sub-committee!
As in the case of corruption as considered in Chapter 12, there is no shortage of people who consider these dealings, even if entirely legal, as immoral. There are politicians who rail against the 'evil capitalists' who 'cheat the poor in developing countries', although their real underlying frustration may be their own inability to control and tax offshore assets. The fact remains that global companies compete, and competition is often stiff. If their shareholders believe the company is under-performing, it

is liable to be taken over, often by a competitor from a different nation (maybe a 'haven') with different legal and moral principles. It is not realistic to expect legally permissible practices of improving profit not to be utilised. It is, however, realistic to expect the concealment of practices that will be seen as hostile by some affected governments and as immoral by idealists and the usual range of opportunistic critics. The concealment brings us immediately into pirate territory. Strict but unofficial oversight is required to ensure that all transactions are executed in the Owner's best interests and, hopefully, without breaking any laws, about which the project team is bound to require reassurance from an expert.

Another job for the Board's Procedural Sub-committee!

20. The Predatory Shareholder

Piracy by Owners

Here is an issue that can't be dealt with by the Director alone, however good his intentions. It is included as a warning to minority shareholders.

What if the pirate is not an executive or entity employed by the enterprise, but is a part of the Owner, i.e. the pirate is a major shareholder or, more likely, a small group of major shareholders? A single majority shareholder is bound to attract attention, including regulatory attention regarding any transactions that may be seen as possibly manipulative. But three, maybe four major shareholders working together behind the scenes … perfect. In the following, we'll call this little group of predators the Cabal.

The Cabal's usual intention is to benefit from share-price values or changes that are unwarranted by actual performance. Note that the profit is mainly or all made at the expense of other past or future shareholders, especially at times of take-over or merger. If there's only one owner/shareholder and no part of the ownership is transferred, none of these issues arises.

Predatory shareholders operate in quite a few different ways, and we are only addressing project-associated piracy. There's downright fraud, in which by countless means a company can be set up and its shares sold or floated at an unreasonably high price. The deception may be carried out by 'salting' a mine, by interfering with the processes of verification of resources, by failure to disclose known risks or liabilities, by inflating the value of a worthless technology, by cooking the books or the prospectus, etc. Generally, such behaviour is supposed to be combated by stock exchange oversight, by financial auditors and by professionals such as police serious frauds offices, and will not be discussed further here.

There are more subtle forms of piracy which may not be classified as criminal. The particular avenue outlined here relates to possibilities for NPV manipulation.

Delusions about Estimate and NPV Accuracy

We have seen in previous chapters how very many assumptions about the future go into the calculation of NPV. These include:

- Forecast capital costs. These can usually be changed by a fairly wide margin, by devices such as reducing capital expenditure at the expense of operating cost (or vice versa), without any change to the forecast operating cost, when factorisation is used to predict operating cost elements, rather than calculation based on actual design. Or the estimate may be adjusted by 'updating' a whole host of uncertainties and assumptions that go into the cost forecast, such as inflation, pricing changes, labour availability, and favourable or unfavourable events and observations as the project progresses. Or contingencies and risk mitigation costs may be reduced by accepting increased risks, or inflated by unjustified allowances.
- Forecast operating costs and revenues. Lying even further in the future than initial capital costs, these are even more subject to a variety of guesses; they include such factors as product prices, input costs, productivity, energy and other efficiencies, etc.
- Financial factors such as interest, discount and foreign exchange rates, and taxation.

As noted previously, it is very difficult to make accurate capital cost comparisons for most large projects, because so often all that is published is a single figure that is easily manipulated. And there is also the case of the self-fulfilling prophecy. From the privately known and published historical data I have accessed, I feel confident to assert that for projects to establish new mines the real range of uncertainty of capital cost estimation is hardly ever better than a band of +/–15%. Note that this can be simply manipulated to be say –20% to +10% by adding an extra 5% contingency. By 'real' range of uncertainty, I mean after attempting to strip away the effect of the self-fulfilling prophecy and similar manipulations, reviewed in Chapter 8, that effectively make the cost outcome more certain, at a higher value. This means a higher cost without any corresponding increase of real value to the Owner.

The same uncertainties, and many more, apply to the operating costs. And usually to the revenues, unless sold forward, in which case cost inflation becomes more of an issue. And to the time of commencement of full production. And … and … and …

Establishing a mine, especially in remote and unfriendly places, has more than its share of difficulties, including necessarily incomplete advance information about what exactly lies underground, and the usually very different design of each mine. Which is probably one of the reasons why Cabals like mining projects. Cabals prefer projects or enterprises where there is a higher degree of uncertainty, something new being done, countries with some lack of government or judicial transparency.

NPV Manipulation

If you have any further use for an author who 'asserts an uncertainty', let me go on to assert that in many projected enterprises the real range of uncertainty of the NPV is not better than +/–20% and often greater. It follows that *without making an error or a demonstrably incorrect calculation or assumption*, it is possible to arrive at an NPV anywhere within this range, depending on the 'view' that is adopted, even by an expert in the relevant field.

In Chapters 5–8, we reviewed various forms of delusion including self-delusion that exist around the subject of cost estimating and control. From this fine range of delusions comes a final and widespread delusion that cost estimating and forecasting is much more accurate than it can actually ever be for most large projects, and especially where there is no closely similar previous project. This includes both capital and future operational cost estimating. It is often very difficult for a project professional, or a consultant who may be employed for a 'due diligence' exercise, to admit to a wider range of uncertainty than the industry is accustomed to be deluded about. I would suggest that the poor fellow (I was once one of them!) often feels obliged to quote a much narrower confidence range than is justified, at risk of being thought to be slack in his workings or professionally incompetent.

A common characteristic of Cabal members is street wisdom. These are people who have a knack of recognising inherently 'grey' or unstable situations and manipulating the circumstances in their favour. They may, for instance, home in on situations featuring challenges that may result in an outcome ranging from high profit to total loss, and set up a 'tails you lose, heads I win' arrangement.

When a project effectively *is* a new enterprise or is a large part of an existing enterprise, the assessed NPV is, apart from current financial assets, the major asset of that enterprise. Here we have a situation where an expert can probably be found to value a company's major asset at a figure that may be substantially higher or lower, without too much risk of being proved to be wrong or deliberately misleading.

I have seen quite a few 'due diligence' exercises that struck me as being poorly performed by individuals rather lacking in insight, and yet the resulting report seemed to be accepted for the purposes of major transactions. When the reality is that there is a high range of uncertainty, such experts may be manipulated by a shrewd operator into coming up with an NPV figure close to the top or bottom of the range of uncertainty. From such practice, opportunity arises to overvalue when selling and undervalue when buying. Take-overs and mergers are ideal occasions to fleece the unwary investor by doing this.

Transfer pricing deals, as outlined briefly in Chapter 19, give similar opportunities to predatory shareholders, if the nominal path of an international transaction passes through an intermediate entity at a profit or loss that is not fully reflected in the project accounts.

Part II. Stopping the Rot

1. The Basic Need

A Summary of the Underlying Problems

Acceptable performance of projects includes, in particular:

1. The pre-project development, evaluation and justification.
2. The choice of optimal alternatives of objectives and how to achieve them.
3. The full definition of the project, and the required constraints and targets.
4. Adequate risk analysis and management.
5. Project authorisation in a fashion whereby its execution is not subject to abuse, and performance incentives are correctly structured.
6. Project execution subject to a verifiable 'best value' strategy.
7. Comprehensive project performance monitoring and reporting systems based on a sound work breakdown structure.

Failure or inadequacy of any one of these major activities leads to a reduction of shareholder value, economic waste and possible damage to third parties and the environment.

In Chapter 7 we arrived at the 'law of business piracy', which is true for all business processes, not only our present subject of projects:

Any business process tends, over the long run, to be abused by the executive responsible for managing it, to the extent that he is able to avoid competition, independent measurement of performance, and accountability.

These three sisters – competition, performance measurement, and accountability – are the nub of the present issue. Take any one of them away, and pirates thrive. They are not unrelated issues: for instance, competition may to a certain extent be a substitute for performance measurement, and vice versa. But competition can easily become destructive and indeed criminal, unless regulated and therefore measured. Performance measurement on its own is futile without a benchmark of acceptability, and competition is usually the best method of setting performance standards.

From this law, it follows that over the long run the value of any organisation owned by third parties is critically dependent on the degree of oversight exercised over the Executive. The routines of governance of companies are reasonably well established as regards their normal business, and continue to receive much attention and development; lately, especially as regards risk management. Even so, there are still shareholder-owned companies with executive chairmen. There are boards whose independent directors have been appointed because their reputations or titles bring credence to an organisation to which they devote little real critical attention. It will be clear from this law that in the long run the Executive of such organisations is liable to gain inappropriate reward and evade performance accountability at the expense of the shareholders. Naturally, many semi-plausible arguments to the contrary will be put forward, but this is what will happen. Only the amount of value lost and of evasion of accountability will vary, and a simple Board Remuneration Committee won't stop it.

Sometimes a Board effectively abdicates its supervisory role and relies almost solely on loosely structured incentives as the means to secure executive performance. This usually leads to the Executive obtaining excessive short-term rewards while the Board has no reliable means of knowing whether performance is sustainable in the long term; whether present profits are being made by mortgaging the future or taking unreasonable risks. The discontinuous nature of a large project especially lends itself to such opportunities for abuse.

The traditional main form of organisational oversight is the auditing of accounts, but that does not work very well for a project. Accounts provide little information about the health of a project until it is finished, and perhaps not even until after a few years of subsequent operation. Professionally executed cost forecasts can provide more useful information, but without marrying them to status reports on schedule, scope and quality adherence the information can be very misleading. Oversight of projects, then, must include technical audit of all of these. The oversight has to be as independent and as professional as a traditional financial audit. Because of the non-steady-state nature of project work, the oversight needs to be carried out much more often than routine financial audits. The Directors need not perform the oversight functions directly, but they must have confidence in the professionalism and independence of the oversight body and must formally accept the oversight reports. It should be clear that an oversight body to which the Project Manager reports cannot fulfil this function, or the oversight body would become part of the Executive and lose its independence.

As outlined in Chapter 9, the oversight of projects has to commence in the pre-project stage, so that project authorisation at Board level can be a one-shot event, without compromising the degree of independent scrutiny, or incurring the costly effects of project delay.

Defining 'Oversight'

The foregoing chapters have outlined several examples of abuse; it remains to summarise the basic methodology for project oversight to prevent abuse and encourage best practice.

The first need is to stress once again that to be effective, oversight has to be a continuing process, commencing well before project authorisation. Published project management literature includes many guides and checklists for 'project audits', and these are widely practised. The concepts of the 'project auditor' and 'project audit' impinge on the field of 'oversight'. Project audit is a part of oversight, but is usually much narrower in its application and offers less immediate benefit to the conduct of the project.

The term 'audit' basically derives from its practice by financial auditors, who have a well-developed and codified methodology. In its application to projects the word can be confusing, creating an expectation that the practice of project audit will be quite similar to financial audit. But there is a significant underlying difference, which is the essential non-steady state of a project; the project work and the critical issues change as the project progresses. This does not lend itself to 'one-shot' auditing, unless the major intention is to retrospectively expose shortcoming and allocate blame, rather than nip inadequate performance in the bud. The project overviewer shares with the financial auditor the need for independence from the Executive, but for effective performance must interact with the Executive and project team almost continually during project conception, authorisation and execution.

I will therefore refrain from using the words 'project audit' or 'auditor' as a substitute for oversight. Audit is only a part of the oversight process and of project quality assurance (QA), which will be discussed further on. I find that I have to use the term 'Overviewer' to describe an individual charged with the oversight role. (The alternative term 'overseer' conjures up visions of a direct controller rather than an observer, even of a man with a whip!) Maybe eventually a professional title will emerge for this role; I know of no other completely suitable title at present.

To be fully effective, the Overviewer (or oversight body) must be completely independent of the Executive. However, there should be a relationship of mutual respect for the necessary close co-operation to develop. An Overviewer who simply issues critical reports to the Owner should be considered to be inadequately performing his function; a critical report needs to be the last resort. The prime credit for project success must go to the Executive and management who drive the project, but some credit should also go to the Overviewer – though not so much that he may be tempted to gloss over under-performance! This is a complex role, calling for maturity rather than any driving personal ambition.

In the following, we will consider, mainly in checklist format, some of the general issues to be addressed by the Overviewer, including any project Owner or non-executive Director who takes on all or part of that role.

2. Reprise: Is the Project Really Justified?

Checklist

In Chapter 2 of Part I, we took an initial look at the examination of project justification. Considerations arising from subsequent chapters are now added to produce a basic checklist:

1. Has the pre-project work been overviewed by the full Board or an independent project auditor, or only by the Executive? If not – and there may be justifiable exceptions, such as clearly attractive opportunities that arise rapidly – the proposal should be viewed with scepticism.
2. Has adequate and verified research been performed to identify alternative competing projects?
3. Can the proposed project reasonably be identified as the best use of capital available? Does it have the highest internal rate of return and attractiveness ratio of known possible competing projects? (See Chapter 4 of Part I.)
4. Other than the quantified financial benefits, what non-quantified benefits to the Owner does or can the project bring, and how will these opportunities be seized? (See Chapter 2 of Part I.)
5. Who else stands to gain by this project, and how will the project investors secure the greater part of these gains for themselves? (See Chapters 1 and 15.)

6. Has the risk analysis and management report been independently reviewed and found to be adequate? (See Chapter 6.)

7. Are there any caveats or disclaimers in the reports and forecasts used to justify the project, and, if so, what will happen if any of the excepted or disclaimed events occur? Is insurance available, and, if not, does this indicate excessive risk? (See Chapter 2.)

8. Considering the financial attractiveness, the non-quantified benefits of the project, and the risks involved, is the Board convinced that the risk/reward ratio is acceptable? Note that projects with a high cost and relatively low NPV seldom prove to be beneficial; they are usually indicators of a fossilised or wrongly focused Executive. High-cost, mediocre NPV, high-risk projects are insane. Non-commercial projects should be appraised very critically. If safety improvement is the objective, consider quantified hazard analysis (Hazan). Require strict quantitative analysis in the case of an environmental project. (See Chapter 17.)

9. Is there an acceptable strategy to obtain best value from project execution? (See Chapter 13.)

10. Has the project been adequately defined over the full life of the investment, with special reference to the presentation of reasonably detailed cost–time and cash flow spreadsheets, and the verification of the match between project scope and future operating costs and effectiveness? (See Chapters 3 and 4.)

11. Have future operational dependencies, such as proposed outsourcing, been carefully analysed to ensure that any dependence on a single-source supplier can be managed? (See Chapters 14 and 15.)

12. Have the targets set out in the project definition and in any incentive schemes been independently reviewed and found to be competitive? (See Chapters 1 and 5–9.)

13. Are any project-related incentive schemes acceptably structured? (See Chapter 1.)

14. Could this be a project with inherently unachievable targets? (See Chapters 1 and 5.) How does any possible failure to achieve the targets match the timescale of accountability of the project Executive and protagonists? Apart from the structure of any

incentive schemes, is the project protagonists' 'money where their mouths are?' (See the note on contractors' accountability below.)

15. Are adequate funds sure to be available as required by the cash flow spreadsheet, including adequate contingencies? There is little that is more damaging to a working project than to run out of funding, or to experience funding delays, and have to suspend work or fail to pay project performers. This often results in the 'fire-sale' of the project asset, and a prescient pirate emerging from the background to snap up a bargain at the shareholders' expense.

Having addressed whether the project is justified in terms of being both a good investment and the best of possible but mutually exclusive investments, we still have to address whether the project has been set up in acceptable fashion. A suitable project charter should be approved before the project's authorisation.

Holding Contractors to Account
Finally, we return to the issue raised in Chapter 1, of project contractors making unachievable promises to land the contract, and then seeking to renegotiate terms once they are entrenched. The only sure way to avoid this is by requiring performance bonds, which need to be:

- of sufficient value to adequately cover the cost of damages the owner may suffer in the event that the contract has to be terminated for non-performance, usually at least 15% of the contract value;
- paid on demand by a first-class bank;
- stringently reviewed by a competent lawyer to ensure that no loopholes exist to let a non-performing contractor off the hook by claiming force majeure or other vague forms of relief.

By corollary, if a major contract is signed without adequate performance bonds, this may well be a sign that an Executive is concealing an unachievable target.

3. The Project Charter

Acceptance of a 'project charter' is an essential part of the project authorisation process. Its prime function is to prescribe how the project will be conducted and controlled. The charter defines the Owner's expectations and target, and thus becomes the document of reference between the Executive and the Overviewer. This target comprises not only what must be achieved, but also what controls must be continually in place to guide and monitor the achievement of the objective. Undoubtedly, different fields of operation require different considerations and emphasis: the following is a basic checklist applicable to most large projects:

- The full project scope and quality definition, embracing everything that will affect operational performance. (See Chapter 3.)
- The project budget (see Chapter 4, noting that for control purposes this cannot be a single figure but must include the cost–time and cash flow spreadsheets). The budget must be supported by a detailed work breakdown, which can be audited to correspond to the detailed project definition.
- The project schedule, including several credible milestones to which progress can be compared.
- Policies and plans for securing 'lateral opportunities' as the project progresses, including where applicable the growth in competence of the Owner's organisation. (See Chapter 16.)

- The constraints within which the project must operate, including safety and environmental plans, government regulations and agreements, taxation, security requirements, asset management requirements. Also ethical practices (see Chapter 12, noting that these may have to be set out in two forms, of which only one is publicly available).
- A full description of how the project will be executed, often called the 'project strategy'. Minimum content includes:
  - Resourcing and procurement plans, for how the various project components, including its management, engineering and direct field cost items, will be acquired and set up to provide the best overall value.
  - A project control plan, including the control of scope, quality, cost, schedule and finance, and how these will be reported.
  - A high-level change control plan, indicating how any proposed changes to the project's delivery will be reviewed and authorised, taking into account the needs of the enterprise as a whole. (See Chapter 3.)
  - The risk analysis and management plan. (See Chapters 6 and 7.) Apart from the major perceived risks, this must highlight any risks, such as force majeure or currency variation, that for whatever reason are excluded from the project targets, and it must detail how such risks will be managed.
  - The project funding plan.

The resourcing and procurement plan mentioned above includes all the project performers and assets deployed from within the Owner's organisation, not just project-specific hire or purchase. It usually excludes the plans to incentivise the top executives responsible, but this is clearly a parallel issue, requiring analysis and oversight as mentioned in Chapter 1.

Most large organisations require some such charter when authorising large projects, though sometimes there is inadequate detail, for instance around some of the points cross-referenced in the checklist in Chapter II.2 above. Worse, this may be covered up by inordinate detail of some of the points which have not been considered worthy of emphasis.

If the charter is non-existent or inadequate in several respects, then the Owner or shareholders may assume they are dealing with a pirate executive.

There should also be an independent oversight charter, drawn up separately by or under the supervision of a Director. This charter and the corresponding oversight has to be in place well before the project is put forward for Board approval, and include the oversight to be exercised to prevent the various forms of piracy mentioned in previous chapters.

Experience indicates that a word of warning is needed about possible 'late changes' to the project charter and its contents during the final project authorisation or initial implementation stages. For a major project, the charter and the issues it addresses will have been developed as an integrated plan, dealing with the major project issues in a mutually consistent fashion. Each component more or less affects each other component. The project execution strategy, in particular, dictates the format of much of the technical specifications, control plans and risk profile. The plans and pre-project documentation for a project foreseen as a single lump-sum turnkey contract are quite different in strategy and format from those for direct work management by the owner's own staff or by a managing contractor. If a late change in strategy is made - for instance, at the Board review and approval stage - this can and often has resulted in an unmanageable project with runaway costs. The financing plan may also have major implications for every aspect of the project's performance.

It is therefore extremely dangerous to approve the implementation of a project subject to alterations whose implications have not been assessed in depth, as may happen if a seemingly attractive project execution 'deal' is concocted, usually by a prospective contractor. The result may be an unbalanced and even unmanageable project.

4. Oversight

The Overviewer or Oversight Body
Summarising and adding to the previous comments, the Overviewer:

- Has to be experienced in the conception and execution of projects similar to those to be monitored.
- Has to report to or be a non-executive director.
- Must not be an egotistical person who wants to show how good he is by showing up the project team (this rules out a lot of otherwise suitable people!), but rather a mature person with whom the project performers will want to work out of respect for his experience. Where possible, the Overviewer should correct suspect or unacceptable practices through quiet interaction.
- Should only report to the Board in writing, and then only after submitting his report firstly to the project management for comment.
- Should be in place at least three months before the authorisation of a major project. No major project should be authorised for execution without considering his report on it.
- Should review the project justification and project charter in depth as soon as they are available. The charter and any revision to it should be subject to his approval.

- Should review and approve the terms of any executive incentive scheme for projects, and ensure that the scheme does not have any failings of the kind outlined in Chapter 1.
- Should review the project status at intervals of one to three months, as may be agreed with the project Executive, depending on the nature of the project.
- Carries no responsibility other than to work professionally. The accountability for project execution remains entirely with the Executive. That means: it will never, ever, be acceptable for the project team to claim they made an error because they did what the Overviewer advised them to do.
- May be one person or a group of people.

Setting up the Oversight

The Board's Overviewer or oversight body may be one or more of its non-executive directors, and perhaps this is to be encouraged if such people have the right experience. But in general, since we are talking about large projects and therefore Boards of major companies or institutions, the Directors are likely to be unable to give adequate attention to the issues that have been raised. Assistance is required.

Some of the major financial auditing firms have set up project consulting divisions that offer oversight services fulfilling at least partially the needs I've outlined; services that are too often limited in scope by an uncomprehending Board. Some of the major business consultants offer services that could be described as overlapping the recommendations made here, but often lacking in some respects, especially those that derive from in-depth knowledge of the practicalities of a specialist business. There are project consultants who offer services to act on behalf of Executives, but they therefore become part of the Executive, not independent of it.

A limitation of many possible consultants is a lack of understanding of the exact workings and mentality of the organisation they are consulting for or reporting on. Sometimes they simply have insufficient appropriate experience and rely too heavily on business school methodologies, rely too heavily on a belief that they can properly understand an established business by observation and talk. The organisations' own executives usually take far longer to gain their eventual best performance than the space of time allotted to such consultants, so surely some comparative lack of insight on the consultants' part is to be expected? Industries and organisations are different from each other. There is not necessarily one unvarying best way of performing work; there are often fundamentally different acceptable ways of achieving the same objective. The 'difference', although sometimes difficult to define, may be one of the most important characteristics of a particular organisation or project team. The way in which a cohesive team of people work with each other can be far more complex than can be set out in a procedure. This is not intended to imply that good consultants cannot be very valuable, since they should bring fresh ideas, knowledge and skills into the organisation; but there is a limit to what they can be expected to achieve, and in fact their achievements can be negative if they lack in-depth knowledge of the organisation in question.

Quality Assurance and Its Limitations

Any major modern project organisation is bound to incorporate QA systems, probably based on the ISO 9000 series standards. Depending on how effectively the QA systems have been set up, these may fulfil many oversight functions and have a major bearing on many aspects of project performance and effectiveness. Thus it is important at this point to examine what QA can be expected to achieve, what it may not achieve in the present context, and how it may be best set up to reduce the burden on the overall oversight function of which it is an important part.

Note that QA systems along ISO 9000 lines are product based, the objective being to assist management to consistently produce the optimal product for the market. 'Optimal' implies the best mix of quality and cost-effectiveness to maximise the long-term profitability of the *operation*, and will usually but not necessarily mean providing the *customer* with the required mix of quality and value. Quality assurance systems are invariably drawn up within the ISO 9000 framework by or for individual companies, or groups of companies, to suit their individual circumstances and methodologies. They are not drawn up by the customer, but most major customers review and approve them before making any commitment.

One of the basics of project management is that work is meticulously planned before commencement. On a well-run project, before any work begins, there is at least an overall framework of how the major work elements will be executed, right up to project completion. Before any individual task commences, there is a plan in place detailing how the work will be performed, to what standards, and how these standards will be assured. All of these plans fall within a set of master-plans or procedures, which become the backbone of the QA system.

ISO 9000 is mainly directed to the needs of organisations that produce simpler products than the management of a large industrial or government project. One of the main differences is that a project management team's immediate product is generally an *interaction* rather than a material entity. It is possible to take a simple view that these interactions are basically presented or confirmed as documents (drawings, specifications, orders, etc.), which are products whose quality is to be controlled, and much project management quality control and auditing is conducted along these lines. This is a necessary but not sufficient condition to ensure that investors are getting what they want.

Because project management has to deal with many situations that are relatively unimportant in most manufacturing situations, in particular the unique circumstances of each project, it is necessary to exercise a degree of interpretation of ISO 9000 when setting up QA for a project. As a result, there tend to be quite surprising differences between the procedural systems of many companies and consultants engaged in project management business.

Most companies get their systems endorsed as compliant with ISO 9000 by accredited independent bodies, but often compliance certificates are issued when the system of procedures is, (in my view at least) seriously deficient in one or more respect. The most frequent such deficiency is that the procedures are not aimed to garner best value from the project's participants, suppliers and contractors. Procurement practice may be allowed to be robotic and bureaucratic rather than embracing well-thought-out strategies that give direction to all aspects of project design and implementation. There may be formal 'value engineering' practices set up to get the best balance between cost and usefulness of all major engineering designs, but insufficient consideration of a best-value strategy for setting up and managing engineering itself.

It is well known that the term 'quality assurance' is something of a misnomer, because no QA system can absolutely assure quality. It can only increase the probability of achieving the desired quality. Actual quality is mainly dependent on the skills, experience and dedication of the producers.

Summarising the observations listed above:

- The customer of a project needs to ensure that the QA systems adopted are right for *his* needs and are structured to assure the delivery of all the requirements of the project charter.
- This is best done by employing an independent Overviewer to review all the major project procedures on which QA is based. This person should have a thorough understanding of the management and execution of the particular type of project (e.g. be a former project manager in the appropriate field). A certificate of compliance to ISO 9000 is on its own likely to be grossly insufficient for this purpose.
- The operation of QA and procedural compliance need to be overviewed throughout the project.
- These actions are still not enough to assure quality on a major project. It is necessary to ensure that the project team is and remains made up of appropriately skilled and dedicated people.

Ex-Corporate Overviewers

What does an organisation do with its older managers and executives when they've passed the point of absorbing stress? Promote them? Early retirement? I would suggest that these people are often the ideal Overviewers. But they *must* first leave the organisation and report to a non-executive Director or chairman. And they *must not* be selected by any Executive. If they are supplemented by consultants from the sources previously mentioned, then perhaps there will be an ideal mix of talent, experience and energy.

Typically, corporate managers are held accountable for everything to do with the way that their departments operate within the organisation. When things go wrong they are inevitably asked, 'Where was your oversight?' Frequently it will be found that they were preoccupied with 'putting out fires' somewhere else in the organisation, or reacting to major unplanned corporate needs; occasionally in this way creating a cycle of fires. This is a typical organisational fault. It is not good management practice to be too dependent on the manager of a department to be also the sole appraiser of the quality of its work. Of course he has to be accountable for the quality of work, or he is accountable for nothing. A corporate quality assurance department may be a wonderful safeguard, but still needs each department head's specialist co-operation to perform properly. This isn't really available, when he is tied up elsewhere by the priorities of the day.

When an executive has more than one responsibility, the organisation should accept that the 'law of multiple objectives' will apply:

> When an executive who is charged with more than one responsibility operates under pressure, his longer-term objectives are likely to be sacrificed in favour of the short-term needs.

This seems to be perfectly obvious to most people, and yet they fail to adequately consider the corollary:

> If a long-term organisational function is important, don't make it the responsibility of an executive who may often be subject to short-term pressures.

The best way of assuring quality performance in the long term is through people who intimately understand the work and its performance, who understand how the organisation interacts and who are not subject to any short-term organisational pressures. A good QA manager, and his assistants, can control procedural adherence, but they cannot usually be expected to judge how well the work is done from a professional specialist's viewpoint. For that you need people accustomed to doing the work – and who no longer have to do it.

Competitors

I have indicated above that, to get the most value out of oversight, it should be performed by a person or body that is sympathetic rather than antagonistic to the project team. It is a mistake to appoint any person or body that competes with or may be seen as competition to the team. The extreme case of this error is to appoint a contractor or consultant to overview the work of a competing contractor or consultant. The desired level of co-operation is bound to be unattainable.

Conclusion: A Cautionary Note for Investors

The issues that have been raised here should make it clear that a corporate executive or government can quite easily abuse projects, whether through deliberate abuse or simply through under-performance. Such abuse may not in the short term or even in the long term be detected by traditional financial audit. There is thus every reason to be wary about the justification, definition and execution of projects and the reporting on their performance, especially in the case of large and complex projects, which are easier to abuse and may lead to more expensive losses.

The only way to combat unacceptable behaviour or performance by any possibly unscrupulous or inadequate project executive (potentially, just about any executive) is to exercise independent oversight of all aspects of the project. Undoubtedly, the techniques and practice of such oversight can be developed much further and more appropriately than has been illustrated, for specific fields of business and government, and for specific applications. Ultimately, it's up to the shareholder, the investment regulator and the voter to control the abuse by insisting on the employment of suitable project oversight.

Oversight costs money, but lack of oversight will almost certainly cost considerably more. Don't be put off by arguments that the oversight will inhibit the performance of the project. It may; but if properly exercised by suitably mature experts, it should rather add value to even well-run projects. It may stop an ill-conceived or ill-executed project in its tracks, and the investor should be grateful for this.

Oversight exercised in a nominal fashion is worse than a waste of money; it leads to deception, including self-deception. It is no good expecting a non-executive director to competently oversee the conception and execution of a large project, if he is paid the same as a director who brings to the Board only his name and his attendance at periodical Board meetings. The Overviewer must receive adequate resources and continuous and full access to information. He must not be paid or employed by the Executive. The shareholders and the regulators need to be convinced of the independence, competence and integrity of the oversight, and the adequacy of the support given to this function.

Failure on the part of Directors to implement adequate oversight of large projects should be seen to be as negligent as running a business without adequate accounts. If there is not an absolute commitment to adequate independent oversight over large projects, don't invest in the enterprise, or don't vote for the government.

Don't make the mistake of assuming that even the most highly qualified financial analysts know how to assess a proposed or actual project. It's a practical matter requiring extensive practical experience.

Investors should be very wary of a project status report that has been prepared by the project team with possible participation of its line management or other interested parties, but not verified by credible independent oversight. A one-shot 'due diligence' review should not be accepted as oversight.

Appendix

Present Value of a Proposed Investment Feature

Derivation of Formulae

Consider an additional project feature that would, if included in the project, reduce operational costs.

P is the present value of the feature (to be calculated).

S is the annual or monthly saving derived from incorporating the feature.

n is the number of years or months over which the feature will be effective.

D is the yearly or monthly discount factor.

Note: D is the ratio of future value to present value, and is equal to $1/(1+d)$ in the formula for NPV, see Chapter 4.

T is the one-shot capital cost of the feature.

Starting from the formula for NPV, Equation (1) in Chapter 4:

$$\text{NPV} = (R_0 - C_0) + \frac{(R_1 - C_1)}{(1+d)} + \frac{(R_2 - C_2)}{(1+d)^2} + \ldots + \frac{(R_{n-1} - C_{n-1})}{(1+d)^{n-1}}$$

For the simplified application, this may be expressed as

$$\text{NPV} = P - T$$

where:

$$P = S + DS + D^2S + D^3S + \ldots + D^{(n-1)}S$$

Multiplying by D,

$$DP = DS + D^2S + D^3S + \ldots + D^{(n-1)}S + D^nS$$

Subtracting the last two equations to sum the series,

$$P - DP = S - D^nS$$

$$\frac{P}{S} = \frac{1 - D^n}{1 - D} \qquad \text{(Equation 2)}$$

This formula is usually used to arrive at a value of P which may be compared with the total capital cost T of the improvement feature, that is, to calculate the NPV. If capital expenditure is spread over a significant period, T should also be discounted, becoming T_D. If investment expenditure is evenly spread over a months or years, then, using the same summation process,

$$\frac{T_D}{c} = \frac{1 - D^a}{1 - D} \qquad \text{(Equation 3)}$$

where c is the mean rate of capital expenditure over period a ($c \times a = T$, the total capital cost arrived at by summing expenditure without regard to time).

The NPV of the feature can now be expressed as

$$\text{NPV} = P - T_D \qquad \text{(Equation 4)}$$

If the savings of operational cost only commence a months (or years) after the capital cost C is incurred, then

$$P = SD^a + SD^{(a+1)} + SD^{(a+2)} + \ldots + SD^{(n-1)}$$

Using the same multiplication and subtraction summation process,

$$\frac{P}{S} = \frac{D^a - D^n}{1 - D} \qquad \text{(Equation 5)}$$

By interpolation, it may be demonstrated that a and n do not need to be integers, but may for instance be years expressed in decimal terms.

If the future savings will increase by an inflation rate of i % per month (or year), then if $j = (100 + i)/100$, and noting that S now becomes the initial rate of savings, the series becomes

$$P = S + DjS + (Dj)^2 S + \ldots$$
From which

$$\frac{P}{S} = \frac{(Dj)^a - (Dj)^n}{1 - Dj} \qquad \text{(Equation 6)}$$

provided always that Dj is not equal to 1, in which case clearly $P = nS$

A Note on Dimensions

Some critics of this analysis are unhappy that the terms P/S and T/S can in customary practice be given the dimensions of time, whereas the right-hand side of the equation is dimensionless. The explanation is that, in deriving the formula, S is the saving in one unit of time, so that strictly P/S and T/S are dimensionless. It is only by extension that we then say we can use the answer as if S were the saving per unit of time. It is easily possible to arrive at false conclusions by, for instance, expressing P/S in years after calculating the value of the right-hand side of the formula in months. Any manipulations need to be made with great care: work either in months or in years. Or, alternatively, forget about the concept of a 'pay-off' period and simply regard these formulae as the means to determine maximum allowable values of P/S, the values of P/S for which the NPV is zero.

The Discount Rate

Further to the observations made in Chapter 4, there are some differences in the practices used by financial analysts to formulate the discount rate, d, from which D is calculated. The discounting practice seems to have derived from the formula used to discount central bank treasury bills, to obtain the ratio of the initial sales price to the value after one year. This does not lend itself readily to the financial situation of most projects, where the requirement is for a cash flow rather than an initial lump sum. Important issues arise from the fact that d is normally expressed on an annual basis rather than the monthly basis on which cash flows are actually controlled and have to be available. The question arises of whether year zero cash flows should not be discounted at all (as reflected in equation 1), or whether they should be discounted by $1/(1+d)$, which would result in Equation 2 changing to

$$\frac{P}{S} = \frac{D - D^{n+1}}{1 - D}$$

This is ultimately a question of definition, which should be resolved as long as there is consistency between the derivation of d and the practice of its application. Given that invariably project cash flows (and interest accruals) are made on a monthly basis, it is arguably better practice that project discounting should be calculated on a monthly basis. The difference to the calculated NPV may be only a few per cent, but 2–3% of a billion dollars is an amount worthy of concern. If we use the NPV calculation as a project control – and, as outlined in Chapters 2 and 3, it is a much more effective control than a value that does not consider discounted cash flow – it is arguably essential to discount on a monthly basis. Failure to do so is likely to create a target ambiguity of a few per cent, which a pirate executive can be sure to use to personal advantage.

Further Possible Refinements
Note that we have implicitly assumed that 'future savings' are based on the premise that the asset performance is maintained by an appropriate maintenance regime, the cost of which has been deducted when calculating the amount of savings. We have also implicitly assumed that the proposed feature will make negligible contribution to the final asset value or decommissioning cost, which is often the case.

If the proposed feature has net residual value X after n months or years, then in determining P the discounted value of X must be added, and following the same summation process, Equation 1 becomes

$$\frac{P - (X \times D^{n-1})}{S} = \frac{1 - D^n}{1 - D} \qquad \text{(Equation 7)}$$

Equations 5–7 can be reworked from first principles to arrive at a general expression:

$$\frac{P - (X \times D^{n-1})}{S} = \frac{(Dj)^a - (Dj)^n}{1 - Dj} \qquad \text{(Equation 8)}$$

The term relating to discounted residual value X often doesn't make much difference to the outcome, unless n is small and X is comparatively large in relation to S. If a is close to zero, then $(Dj)^a$ can be taken as 1.

Performing to a Specified Internal Rate of Return

For this criterion, all that needs to be done is to replace the discount rate d by the required rate of return r, such that D becomes $1/(1 + r)$.

Performing to a Specified Attractiveness Ratio

In Chapter 3 we defined the attractiveness ratio e of a proposed investment as

$$e = \frac{NPV}{NPV_0}$$

Like a specified IRR, this can be used to settle the question of 'How much better than the pay-off period does the feature's P/S ratio need to be to make the feature worthwhile?' In effect, the overall availability of funding (or the capacity of the organisation to carry out projects) is taken into consideration, not just the opportunity cost of funding as indicated by the discount rate or the required rate of return.

To perform to a specified attractiveness ratio, we shall consider the case in which there are no revenues or benefits until the project has been completed a months or years after starting. From then on monthly or yearly cost savings (or alternatively net revenue increases) are available at a rate S, calculated at pre-project prices.

Because there are no revenues before project completion, NPV_0 is equal to T_D, the discounted capital cost. Combining the definition of e with Equation 4,

$$NPV = P - T_D$$
$$NPV = e \times NPV_0 = e \times T_D = P - T_D$$

Therefore

$$P = T_D(1 + e)$$

Substituting this value into Equation 8,

$$\frac{T_D(1 + e) - (X \times D^{n-1})}{S} = \frac{(Dj)^a - (Dj)^n}{1 - Dj}$$

which may be rearranged as

$$\frac{TD}{S} = \frac{(Dj)^a - (Dj)^n}{(1 - Dj)(1 + e)} + \frac{(X \times D^{n-1})}{S(1 + e)} \qquad \text{(Equation 9)}$$

Note that the term $(X \times D^{n-1})$ will often be negligible and taken as zero, and a can often be taken as zero, in which case $(Dj)^a = 1$.

To evaluate e for given values of T_D, S, D, j, a and n, Equation 9 may be rearranged as

$$e = \frac{S}{T_D} \times \frac{(Dj)^a - (Dj)^n}{(1 - Dj)} + \frac{(X \times D^{n-1})}{T_D} - 1 \qquad \text{(Equation 10)}$$

Example

A project has been proposed to build a power station. The project may be enhanced by adding features such as additional feed heaters, to provide greater thermal efficiency with increased capital cost. What is the maximum pay-off period T_D/S to satisfy the following criteria?

Period of construction $a = 4$ years
Operational life until decommissioning = 25 years, from which $n = 29$ years
Required attractiveness ratio $e = 0.2$
Discount rate d = 8%
Inflation rate $i = 4\%$
There is negligible residual value after 25 years' operation, after allowing for decommissioning costs.

Answer

$D = 1/(1 + d) = 1/1.08 = 0.926$
$j = (1 + i)/100 = 1.04$
$Dj = 0.926 \times 1.04 = 0.963$

Note that, in this case, S becomes the increase of annual operational return if the proposed feature is incorporated.

$$\frac{T_D}{S} = \frac{(Dj)^a - (Dj)^n}{(1 - Dj)(1 + e)} + \frac{(X \times D^{n-1})}{S(1 + e)} \qquad \text{(Equation 9)}$$

$$\frac{T_D}{S} = \frac{(0.963^4 - 0.963^{29})}{(1 - 0.963)(1 + 0.2)} + 0 = 11.9 \text{ years}$$

T_D/S has to be less than 11.9 years for the required attractiveness ratio to be met.

Or, alternatively, to evaluate e from given T_D/S, use Equation 10.

Residual Value

By comparison, if the residual value X is 20% of the inflated initial value T_D, then after 29 years

$$X = 0.2 \times T_D \times 1.04^{(29-1)} = 0.62 \times T_D$$

Using this we can calculate the term in Equation 9 relating to residual value X

$$\frac{(X \times D^{n-1})}{S(1 + e)} = \frac{(0.62 \times T_D \times 0.926^{28})}{S \times 1.2} = 0.06 \times \frac{T_D}{S}$$

Incorporating this into Equation 9,

$$\frac{T_D}{S}(1 - 0.06) = 11.9$$

$$\frac{T_D}{S} = 12.7 \text{ years (an increase of 6\%)}$$

Conclusion

Use of these formulae for other than a quick 'reality check' on a proposed scoping decision may seem to be rather superficial in the context of a very expensive project, but such checks are often useful for oversight purposes. In practice, there may be a professional economic evaluation service available to determine and implement the required project economic criteria. That's excellent – provided that this service is correctly linked to the realities of the project and is not subject to manipulation by interested parties. The considerations listed above should still help the project Overviewer to ensure that the eventually agreed criteria are comprehensive, logical and properly applied. Many major projects are still being executed in which the only regard paid to possible operational cost savings and performance improvements is the vague statement that 'naturally there will be some future improvement projects paid for out of operational revenue'.